A Different Metaphor

Faith That Imagines the Impossible

A Different Metaphor

Faith That Imagines the Impossible

Kevin Shinn

Lincoln, Nebraska

ISBN 979-8-9851689-2-1 (print edition)

Published by 55 Degrees Publishing.

Printed in the United States of America.

To Shade Tree

9/18/1985

Surely you will summon nations you know not,
and nations you do not know will come running to you,
because of the Lord your God,
the Holy One of Israel,
for he has endowed you with splendor

Isaiah 55:5

Contents

All Illustrations by Annika Kristin

Annika is an artist residing in and taking inspiration from her home in Nebraska. I met her randomly on Instagram as I was drawn to the simplicity of her craft. I mistakenly thought she was a friend of my daughter, so I reached out to her to tell her how much I loved her work. She responded graciously and asked if I ever needed a commission, she would love to create something for me.

Keys are an important icon to me, so I asked her to do something around the topic of keys. About two weeks later, a box arrived in the mail and it was the image on the front cover. I was moved to tears at how she had interpreted the image. Take a close look at the picture and see if you can see what she did.

I showed my daughter the art and told her that Annika had drawn them. She said, "Dad, I don't know that woman."

This is one reason why I don't believe in coincidence.

Follow her work at Instagram.com/annikakristin_illustration

All Photography by Ike Somanas

Ike is an aspiring chef, filmmaker, and photographer. I met Ike through my restaurant, and he has served as my sous chef. We both enjoy collaboration on artistic projects, and his skillful eye captured the images exactly as I imagined them looking.

Follow his work at www.ikesomanas.com
Or at Instagram.com/ikesomanasphoto

Acknowledgments

Thanks to Cindy Conger, The Champion of Authors. You certainly live up to your title.

Thanks to Phil Whitmarsh for helping me get this book across the finish line.

Thanks to Dan Parson for always starting conversations for me that I would have never started on my own.

FOREWORD

BY TONY GOINS

I often describe Kevin as my "pastor", my brother, my friend, and the man that has literally prayed life into my life. He's my confidant, and I trust him implicitly with all aspects of my being. When you read about the mighty influences in the Bible, add Kevin Shinn's name to the list. Words alone can't begin to explain my agape love for Kevin. During the most challenging times in my life, Kevin made time and supported me. God sent him to earth to spread his messages of love, forgiveness, and redemption. His exploration of faith not as a rigid set of beliefs but as a dynamic and evolving force resonated with my own experiences in the ever-changing business world. Kevin and I bonded first over food and cigars. This was God's plan to create this amazing relationship between the two of us.

Shinn's honesty and vulnerability in sharing his own journey of faith and doubt reminded me that even the most successful leaders have moments of uncertainty and that it's okay to question and explore new ideas.

"A Different Metaphor" is a book that will stay with me long after I've finished reading it. It's a call to action to embrace change, find our own voices, and imagine the impossible, both in our personal lives and in our businesses. Let me close by saying this; Kevin's book is a must read and will inspire continual transformation in your life.

Sincerely,
Tony Goins

PRELUDE

The vistas I see are a direct result of the shoulders I stand on. My perspective, my point of view, even my sense of humor have been influenced by those who came before me. I felt it necessary to acknowledge a few people at the outset of this book. These are the authors who have shaped this book you are about to read.

In 1998, I encountered the work of Dallas Willard in his incredible book, *The Divine Conspiracy*. It came to me at a time of deep soul-searching and provided a new metaphor for the beatitudes in Matthew 5. I was always taught that the beatitudes are a checklist of how to be blessed, but Dr. Willard introduced the idea that there is nothing on this list to which to aspire. Instead, he describes the beatitudes as an invitation, a guest list, if you will, of the people who are also invited to share in the Kingdom of Heaven. The poor in spirit, the meek, the perfectionists who are pure in heart—they get the same invite. Being blessed has nothing to do with performance or achievement. It's all about the Son of Man who has come to disrupt the world and change its rules entirely.

This was the invitation I was looking for but had no idea was possible. And it took the voice of a man like Dallas Willard to make his thoughts available to someone like me. I am forever grateful to him.

Not long after, John Eldredge published his book, *The Journey of Desire*. I picked up a copy in the Spring of 2000 and couldn't put it down once I opened it. Here was another writer describing a vision of the human experience I had felt in my heart but didn't have the words to articulate. He was the first man of faith I encountered who didn't dismiss the heart as deceitful and wicked. Instead, Eldredge pointed out that by faith, the heart is made new again and thus should not be feared. Our desires are not impulses to be shamed but now are motivations to be explored and understood. The thoughts in this book aided me as I considered making a major career change in 2004. I trusted my heart to move in an entirely different direction.

In the Spring of 2020, soon after my wife died, I boarded a plane to Ireland. I love all things Irish and felt The Emerald Isle would understand my grief. Among the things I packed, I placed a copy of John O'Donohue's book of poetry, *To Bless the Space Between Us*. I didn't read it on the plane. Instead, I waited until I was in country to open it. One morning on a train to Waterford, I pulled the book from my backpack and started reading.

And the tears came.

I couldn't believe what I was reading. I had never encountered poetry like this before. The author was pouring out blessing after blessing over my deep sense of loss. And I didn't even get past the first five poems. This book was my invitation to begin writing poetry.

There are other influences I could list, but these three men have had a direct impact on me as I write this book. And I need to give credit where credit is due.

When I first started writing, I learned years ago not to worry about the audience and what it thinks. This is important because I cannot control what my audience sees, hears, or thinks. My job as a writer is to be as clear as possible and make my words available, with the hope that someone might say the same thing I did about Willard, Eldredge, and O'Donohue.

INTRODUCTION

I recently watched a TikTok reel produced by a YouTuber who would be in the category of discernment ministry. These are folks who have it as their mission to point out error, heresy, and false teaching in the Church as We Know It. He showed a short clip of a sermon given by an LGBTQ pastor who made a statement that God is gay, God is lesbian, God is trans, God is cisgender, and so on. The YouTuber's response was so intriguing and thought-provoking. He vehemently said, "I believe if Jesus were here today, he would spit in the face of this man's theology!"

Spit in the face?

This is strong language and provocative imagery with which I am not comfortable. But looking through the comment section on the YouTuber's reel, this kind of language is perfectly fine with a whole lot of people. I am not writing to them. I'm not out to start an argument with anyone. To the minds that are fixed and made up, I say, "So be it." I don't seek to correct, cajole, or condemn another person's faith. Who among us knows the thoughts of a person but that person alone? I am not the judge and jury.

It's hard for me to picture Jesus spitting in the face of a controversial person, especially one in need of kindness. There is that one instance where Jesus spit on the ground, but that was to make a poultice out of dirt to rub on the eyes of a blind man so he could see again. But spitting because of difference? I'm just not sure which of the gospels this man has been reading to create a belief that spitting was an appropriate response to disagreement with someone.

What would it mean to spit in the face of this man's theology?

Spitting on someone or something implies more than just anger. Spitting is an act of disdain and contempt. There is rage involved in demeaning someone in this way. And where does that rage come from? Is it righteous indignation? Is it justifiable violence in the name of orthodoxy? Is it all a part of fighting the good fight in order to defend the faith against false doctrine and its teachers? Could it be fearful discomfort?

It's this kind of language that stirred me to begin to write. The YouTuber's statement was so provocative to me that I have not been able to let it go.

Why does this bother me?

It bothers me because the language is unproductive and unhelpful for me as I seek to communicate an image of who my Maker is and how I have grown to be enamored by The One Who Created Me. It's incendiary and is not congruent with the new-wine faith that I have begun to drink. I need a new wineskin to contain it all.

It is not the type of language in which my faith now thrives.

REASON FOR WRITING

As with most of my writing, I write for myself first. Everything I post or print is a series of thoughts that started in my heart and mind as a struggle or personal observation. It's why I so often write in the first person. I am my primary audience as I flesh out these new ideas.

I also write to those who might be like me. I am a person who embraces a long-standing faith tradition but is uncertain about continuing along the specific path on which I was led to express it. This group is often called deconstructionists. These are folks who are unsettled about their faith and are ready to tear it down and go in another direction, which I don't think is a bad thing. All faith needs to be disrupted in some fashion in order to prove what it is made of. If the Good News is good, it should be able to withstand some shaking and quaking along the way.

But I also write to people who realize the faith language that was handed to them is inadequate to express their newfound amazement and the beauty of their new discoveries about Jesus. As faith burgeons, so must the language that contains it. An expanding faith needs an ever-expanding vernacular that tells its story.

I seek a different metaphor than spitting.

This is why I believe written language is not enough. What if a person can't read? Are they disqualified from the life of faith the Holy Spirit wants to fan into flame? The body is more than the cognitive, rational brain. It is life, spirit, emotion, movement, and sensation. It's why music and poetry and ritual need to be added to the dialect of faith. These three art forms say more than words alone.

I titled this book *A Different Metaphor* because I needed one. I needed different pictures and imagery. I'm confused by the metaphor of spitting in the face. I want something bigger, broader, and more in line with how I see the person of Jesus. I see him engaging someone different than he, not dismissing them. I picture an inquisitive and curious person because, admittedly, I'm not a confrontational person. And I will admit my bias. I'm a lover, not a fighter. I am drawn to words that describe the metaphor of the former, not the latter.

But bias is baked into every equation. For every person committed to thinking "biblically" about a matter, countless others will disagree with their view or conclusion, using the very same Bible. No one is fully objective and neutral. Nor should we be. Disagreement adds color and texture to the dialogue of faith. If everyone thought alike that would make lots of us unnecessary. And I would argue we need that bias for our faith to thrive. Faith is being assured of what we hope for. I'm not sure we all hope for the same thing in the same way.

I remember when the What Would Jesus Do? (WWJD) movement came along. It was an interesting viral water cooler topic that encouraged people to stop and ponder what Jesus might do in a particular situation and try to imitate that. It's a good question, but I admit, most of the time I have no idea what he would do. I am also cautious about trying to get him on my side of an issue because I have a feeling I would be on the wrong end of the assumption.

One goal I have for myself as a writer is to use my voice to help you hear yours. I might say something that you have felt but didn't have the words to express. Or I might bring up a subject that you disagree with, and it was that disagreement that led you to formulate your own thoughts and convictions about the matter. I don't seek agreement, but I do hope I can make my point clear, even if you think I am way off.

Here's to finding different metaphors and to new wineskins for all the new wine with which your faith will fill them.

KS

If you find it hard to hear and understand
Keep in mind
That English
Isn't the son of man's
First language

The son of man
Has an innate love
Of communication
And sometimes
Goes by the name
Word

Hearken to the light
That surrounds you
Give ear
To the scope of the sky

Notice the articulation
Of the songbird
And how the moon
Enunciates
Through its glow

Concentrate
On the way
The cloud forms
Take heed
Of the voice
Of the prairie

Watch the trees speak
And how the rocks
Cry out
Absorb
Each statement
From the mountains
And the hills

The beautiful fluency
Of nature
Will never
Be speechless

Some of us

Didn't need

A new faith

We just needed

A different metaphor

Chapter 1

My Foundations of Faith

Seminary Isn't for Everyone

Growing up in Oklahoma, I was raised in the faith of the Southern Baptist tradition. Its main earmarks were often stated and well-ingrained. It seemed like every Sunday, I heard about heaven and hell, why I needed to get saved and be baptized, and, if I were really serious about the Savior, I would be in attendance everytime the church doors were open.

As a young man, I didn't have an issue with any of this. I didn't know I could. I went along as I was taught and did what I was told. It wasn't until I entered a Southern Baptist seminary that everything began to come into question.

On my first day of class, I met Professor Cate, whom everyone referred to as Dean Cate because he was dean of students. (It took me about half the semester to realize his first name wasn't Dean.) He gave the most memorable lecture of my entire formal theological education. In a fatherly, professorial tone, he said to the class:

"Some of you are going to find out very quickly that seminary education is not for you."

Quite a statement by the man who was considered the students' pastor.

He wasn't being mean or hard-nosed. He was being honest, speaking from years of experience, seeing a new class of seminarians enter another school year and watching the same attrition rate as before. Students leaving the institution was nothing new to him. His wisdom allowed him to watch and pay attention. He was always ready to offer a kind word to those who decided to pack it in and move on.

In his opening lecture, he pointed out that theological education is academic and not devotional in nature. The academic disciplines can be stimulating and demanding, but they can also be cold and distant. He said his best-case scenario is both/and. Vigorous study of theology should always lead to kindness and compassion, not smug indifference toward those who hold a different view.

Dean Cate also noted that many in this classroom would not last a month, because the faith they brought in with them was not ready or even meant to be challenged the way it was about to be. But he was careful to add that it didn't mean their faith was illegitimate or less than. Faith isn't meant to be a contest; it is highly personal, being both objective and subjective.

He was the professor who taught me the importance of making room for mystery and dissonance. "Your congregations are going to be full of people who don't really care about the tense of that Greek verb. They want to know how they are going to deal with their suicidal child."

I wish I had gotten to know Dean Cate better. I wish I could go back and bring all the new questions with me and see what he has to say about them. He was one of those people who had an endearing presence. He taught theology and doctrine in such a way that led me to believe he was a man of deep faith—a faith I wanted to emulate.

And this is the point I want to make in this book: As I understand the scriptures, faith is the one thing that matters and merits my full attention. Galatians 5:6 states it this way:

> *For in Christ Jesus neither circumcision nor uncircumcision has any value. The only thing that counts is faith expressing itself through love.*

Doctrine and theology are nothing without being surrounded by faith expressing itself through love. Dean Cate reinforced that to me as a twenty-four-year-old seminarian. And now, as a man in midlife, I still hold his example close to my heart. I want to be known as a man with faith worth imitating. The writer of Hebrews says:

> *Remember your leaders, who spoke the Word of God to you. Consider the outcome of their way of life and imitate their faith.*
>
> Hebrews 13:7

I write this book as an act of faith, in hopes that it will become a catalyst for the faith of others. I take the steps to assemble the thoughts I have in my heart as if I am putting together a jigsaw puzzle. My words are the pieces, and the picture becomes clearer as I write and set them in place.

Why I Had to Leave the Ministry to Find My Faith Again

Change That Invigorated My Faith

After I graduated from seminary, I took a position as a collegiate pastor in Nebraska. I sent down roots very quickly and embraced the work in front of me. My primary role in the ministry was as a worship leader. (For those who are not familiar with church structure, I was the person who led the music for the congregation to sing along with before the pastor got up to preach the sermon.) This was a time when church music was not performed by a live band. Most of the time, someone on a piano or guitar led the music, and the production and setup were minimal. But around 1988, I started to catch wind of a growing movement in churches around the country. At that time, this movement was emanating mostly from charismatic denominations. Music in these churches started sounding like what was on the radio because it was led by a lead singer in a rock-and-roll band, not a conductor with a keyboard or pipe organ.

Many credit this proliferation to the Vineyard movement, an association of churches started in 1982 in Southern California by a musician named John Wimber. John was the keyboard player for The Righteous Brothers and was eventually inducted into the Rock and Roll Hall of Fame in 2003. He introduced the form and style of music he was most comfortable with to The Church as We Know It. And this change was significant.

As with any change, this shift was held in suspicion. The complaints were myriad. Old folks thought it was too loud. Others decried it as all emotionalism and a pretentious show. Some even accused it of being demonic. I faced my share of these criticisms as I explored this new expression of church music. Working with college students was a little different. They did not have the trappings of tradition to hold on to. They were early adopters of this new style of music and received it with vigor.

Very early on, I formed a little band of student musicians in our ministry, and we started to feel this wind of change blowing through our group immediately. What I witnessed in them was a congruence between their thoughts, beliefs, and emotions. The students were now given permission to feel their faith in God and not just ascend to it intellectually. They could express their devotion in a more powerful way through music than just processing it through spoken or written words.

Our little band started getting requests to go to other campuses and lead worship experiences. There were moments of transcendence during these gatherings where it felt like time had stopped and the Divine Presence entered the room. There were times when silence was the best response to what was happening, and the band would stop playing to allow for The Unseen Voice to sing and play. I felt so honored to be involved in such powerful moments.

Change That Discouraged My Faith

But within a few short years, the landscape started to change again. Now, having a rock-and-roll band in a church or student ministry was a necessity. Congregants and attendees began to expect a higher level of musicianship and professional production values in what was presented on Sunday mornings and at weeknight student gatherings. Worship bands got bigger and better and louder and started producing and recording original songs for sale and distribution. A subtle, insidious, and competitive spirit emerged among the student groups. The question of who had the better band influenced how students decided where to attend.

I could acutely feel this new demand. It affected how worship was implemented. An intangible element was missing when I led music, and I could not put my finger on it. I could only speak of what I was witnessing. My joy started to diminish, and this troubled me. I continued in my position but with waning interest and enthusiasm. I could tell I was beginning to go through the motions of ministry. There was nothing fresh or new in me.

The final straw that broke the camel's back was when I was preparing to give a talk at the beginning of a new semester. In my preparation, it dawned on me that I was getting ready to tell the same set of fifteen-year-old stories. I was about to introduce another new class of students that arrived on campus every year in August to the same illustrations I had been telling from the beginning. This bothered me deeply. Why didn't I have new stories? I wondered where the new stories were and what it would take for me to find them.

I didn't have new stories because I didn't have new faith to generate them.

Until then, I had made some significant choices by faith to explore the new things I was discovering. I chose to move to Nebraska because I saw it as a step of faith. I remember the exact day I made the decision. It became clear when I was weighing out the pros and cons of uprooting from my familiar heritage to go to an unknown place. The list of pros for moving was so much longer than staying put. And when I said aloud, "The only reason I wouldn't move is because I am afraid to," I could see clearly. I could tell it was the right decision. It was right because it required faith.

In the same way, in 1990, as I watched the modern worship movement burgeon, I could discern it was something worth exploring but would require faith to do so. I decided by faith to hop on board that train. It required risk to go against the norms of The Church as We Know It but the reward was worth the initial discomfort from naysayers.

Fast forward to 2003. It had been over a decade since I had taken similar faith steps. As I grew more honest with myself, I knew I was getting stagnant in my faith because there were no choices to kindle it. I could feel a new choice was coming. Was I ready to deliberate and consider?

Finding Much-Needed Inspiration

I had been dreaming about owning a restaurant for several years. I can show you a journal entry from December 1994, when I first began writing about it. I had just attended a national student conference in Louisville, Kentucky, where one of the keynote speakers was Tom Sine. I was looking forward to hearing him speak since I was familiar with his book, *Mustard Seed Conspiracy*, published during my freshman year of college in 1981.

He introduced his message with a description of the oncoming postmodern generation that no one in The Church as We Know It knew anything about. He sketched a little illustration to explain. On the lower left corner of the white-board, he drew a box with a cross on top. This, he said, was the church contained in the four walls. He pointed out that many in this audience would find their best expression of faith within this box. The way the church is structured, organized, and expressed in its current form made sense to this group of people.

He then drew a diagonal line toward the middle of the board. In the center, he made an underscore as if it was a blank on a written test. Sine said there were also people in this audience who would find their best expression of faith outside the four walls by moving to a place that fills in the blank of what is missing. He encouraged this group of people to believe in the vision they carry and engage their faith to create what is needed.

He then drew another diagonal line toward the top right corner of the whiteboard. This arrow pointed to a question mark. He paused, looked intently at the audience, and said something that shook me to my core.

"Some of you are called to a place you don't even know if it can exist or not."

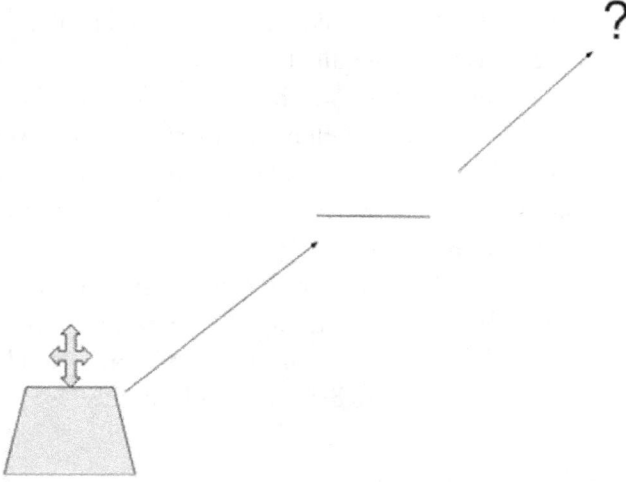

As he described this third expression of faith, it felt like he was speaking directly to me. I thought someone was validating the unsettledness in my soul. I wasn't comfortable with fifteen-year-old stories. I didn't like what was becoming of the modern worship movement that was rapidly morphing into something that no longer resonated with me.

Why My Faith Was Not Thriving

On the way home from Louisville, I started journaling about this experience. I started my writing with this question:

> *Why are my best conversations with people in settings of hospitality where there is food, alcohol, and music?*

My question came from the many Thursday nights talking with students in a local pizza bar after our weekly college ministry meetings. It came from the honest moments with a friend struggling in his faith or marriage over a pint of ale. It was the time after the concert to stop off at a pub when we weren't ready for the evening to end because the music was so memorable that it needed a conversation to punctuate it.

Why were these stories so much more prevalent and quicker to recall than stories within the four walls of The Church as We Know It? Tom Sine's insight became a catalyst for my thinking and contemplation, even though it would take seven more years for me to take the next step of faith. I continued to dream about the restaurant and wondered if this was part of filling in the blank that Sine outlined. Or was it further toward the question mark of existence in his illustration?

I like to think of this season as seven years of germination. Like a seed, it took that long for the picture of a restaurant to start swelling and pushing against the outer shell that covered it. The seed of an idea always experiences pressure as it grows into its potential. This was no different.

It wasn't an easy season. I was filled with self-doubt. I wrestled with guilt and shame in the process. I wondered if I was falling away. Was I taking my hand from the plow and turning back? Was I abandoning my work for selfish reasons? Maybe I should just stick it out and call it being faithful.

But therein was the Catch-22. To stay put could mean being faithful to the work I was engaged in. It could mean that I need not grow weary in the doing of good, knowing that in time, I would find my reward for it. But it could also mean that there was very little faith in staying faithful. I believe every step of faith will have these two sides to it. There will always be a choice, and many times that choice isn't clear-cut.

The Wild Goose

Early Celtic Christians likened the Holy Ghost to a goose. Unlike the dove, which is gentle and a symbol of peace, the goose is a bit more untamed and unpredictable. And there have been times in my experience that living a life of faith feels like a wild goose chase. I'm not always sure where I'm going, but if I do well to stay close and follow the honking, I'm sure to be led into a new adventure, whatever it might be.

I describe my choice as having to leave the ministry to find my faith again. It was evident that it was not thriving within The Church as We Know It. Just as Dean Cate pointed out on that first day of seminary, some folks will not thrive in an academic setting. Just because a person didn't fit at seminary doesn't imply their faith is inferior; it only means that they are not inclined to express their faith within that place. And for Dean Cate to offer liberty to his students in helping them discover this distinction increased my respect for the man.

I heard Sine offering me the same permission. Faith is not monolithic in its expression. The very essence of faith is being sure of what is unseen. The person who has the faith to envision the better future within the four walls of The Church as We Know It should do so with the same enthusiasm as the person who believes they are destined to fill in the blank on Sine's illustration.

I knew in my spirit that I was one of those people Tom Sine was talking about who didn't fit within the four walls. But I wanted a sense of being released from the current assignment before embarking into the great unknown. I didn't want to make a major decision that would disrupt my family without feeling like I was moving toward something, and not just away from something because of my angst.

I finally received that permission in an unusual way.

A Most Important Vision.

As I said earlier, I knew I had to leave the ministry in order to find my faith again. But it was important that I had a sense of blessing and permission from The Comforter before I made such a decision. My faith was not thriving, and the most compulsive idea I had at the time was to step out in faith and build the restaurant I had been dreaming of for several years. On paper, this decision seemed foolish. I had no restaurant experience. I had never worked as a chef. Never been to culinary school. But I knew how to cook for people, and, more importantly, I knew how to create a hospitable space for them to feel welcome and cared for. This was the congruent piece in the transition from ministry to hospitality. I was still putting myself in a position to take care of people.

For some reason, I did not write the exact date on this journal entry, but I had the vision sometime late in 2003. The terrorist attacks on the World Trade Center towers two years prior had rocked me to the core of my being. I thought to myself, "Here I am, the guy paid to have the answers and shepherd the flock, left with no sense of anything right." I felt like I was on a leaky liferaft adrift on a rough sea. I knew I couldn't be of help to anyone in this condition. I thought if you were drowning too, might as well hop aboard, and we'll both sink together. That was my mentality.

One morning, while still in bed, a very specific vision started to play out in my mind. The setting was in the office of the church building I once attended. I was preparing for band practice that evening and was collating sheet music and chord charts for the music team. As I was standing at the copier, I looked out the window toward the south lawn and saw a person standing in the distance. The person began to wave at me to come outside. I left everything at the copy machine and walked out the front door to see who this was and what he wanted.

As I got closer, I saw it was the Son of Man who had been waving at me. He had a big smile on his face, and he was holding a ring of keys in his right hand. They were vintage skeleton keys of differing shapes and sizes. He asked me how I was doing, and I told him, "Not very good." He totally ignored my answer and continued to smile and look me in the eye.

To cut the awkwardness, I asked him what he had in his hand. He held the ring of keys out to me and said, "These are the keys to men's hearts. I want to give them to you and teach you how to set people free." He put them in my hand, and the next thing he said startled me.

"Now don't go back into that building. Go that way." And he pointed to the western horizon.

And thus, the vision was complete.

I remember the feeling of surprise, knowing I had just received something important. I got out of bed and wrote it down. Was this my permission that I had been waiting on? I would hold on to it and wait and see. I took the major pieces of this visual story and reflected on them. The sense of dullness in me. The enthusiasm on the face of Jesus. His excitement in handing me the ring of keys. The assignment of setting others free. His instruction not to go back into that building. All of this was to direct me to a place where my faith would thrive again. He pointed west. A general direction. Nothing specific or step-by-step. Trust was implied, and his belief in me was bestowed.

That's how I knew I could trust it. Everything was in line with who I know my Maker to be. And my faith wanted to stretch and move again. It was time to lace up and run.

I kept it to myself, except to share it with the Man of God, who always knows what to do with my dreams and visions. I gave it a few months, and my heart became more excited about it. This was more confirmation that it was time to take the step of faith toward the unknown and launch the restaurant. In 2004, I announced my resignation for May 2005. I would finish out the school year and help ensure a smooth transition. I was as ready as I ever would be.

The power of a personal vision like this can be seen as an anchor that keeps the ship from drifting when circumstances start going badly. After I resigned and was in the process of looking for new income, my wife lost her job. The stress of unemployment for both of us was compounded by my dad passing away two months later. It was very easy to assume I had made a huge mistake and would have been better off staying put. A commitment to faith benefits from a visual picture like a dream or vision. It can serve to remind us why the decision was made in the first place.

I want to be clear that I am not assuming that my story should be normative for all people of faith. Visions cannot be manufactured or drummed up.

But if you have been gifted in this way, I hope my words can help explain what you might encounter if you choose to step into discerning your gift by faith.

My bias toward metaphor has required a step of faith to lean into them. In addition to inviting dreams and receiving visions, I allow the beauty and importance of physical icons, like keys, songbirds, and hinges. I will explain later how these symbols encourage my faith to keep moving toward that place I'm not certain can exist.

Personal Metaphors

For years, the Holy Spirit has spoken to me in dreams and visions. These experiences are types of metaphors. They are filled with pictures and imagery that communicate a message to me. Pictures are easier to remember than words. It's why you can remember someone's face but quickly forget their name, so when you see that person again days later, you might recognize their image but not their name. My dreams and visions are like that. To be given a visual story makes it easier to attach my faith to its message and begin to act on it.

Dreams

And here is the context of how that plays out in my faith. I distinguish the two like this: A dream is a story or image that is played out in my mind during sleep. These pictures are often disjointed and include characters who are unrelated to each other. But the common thread of a dream is the emotion that surrounds it. For example, I might have a dream about my next-door neighbor driving away in my new 2023 Ford F-150. I don't pay attention to the details, especially since I don't own a 2023 Ford F-150. Instead, I pay attention to the emotion I am feeling, which is anger at the neighbor for borrowing my truck without my permission.

To make sense of the dream, I started with how I was feeling. Because I had been doing therapy work to resolve past repressed memories, I recalled feeling resentment toward that neighbor who had been rude to me over the years. This makes the dream a valuable tool for understanding and restoration.

Solomon noted this in Ecclesiastes 5:3:

> *For the dream comes through much effort and the voice of a fool through many words.*

Whatever dominates our thoughts will be the subject of our dreams. When I was in the market to buy my first house, I dreamed about houses nightly. This effort, as Solomon says, revealed itself in my dream.

The value of a dream is found in the body's ability to reveal hidden thoughts and emotions. It is a remarkable gift and another beautiful way Our Creator speaks to us. A dream is crucial data for those of us who have them. But if you don't dream or can't remember your dreams, don't worry about it; you probably aren't wired to tune into that frequency.

To be clear, I don't believe all dreams and visions have great spiritual significance. But they do have value in revealing insight into what our heart is needing. Sometimes they can show us that our bodies are stressed and need more sleep.

Visions

The second means of communication from My Creator is through visions. I distinguish a vision from a dream this way: as the dream is played out during sleep, a vision comes to me during wakefulness or at that point of transition in or out of sleep. Daniel described it this way:

> In the first year of Belshazzar king of Babylon, Daniel saw a dream and visions in his mind as he lay on his bed; then he wrote the dream down and related the following summary of it.
>
> Daniel 7:1

Here the words dream and vision are used interchangeably, but both distinctions can still apply. Daniel was at a state of rest when he received these messages.

When I have been given a vision, here is what I do with it:

1. **First and foremost, assume it is for me.**

   If something troubling or outrageous shows itself in a dream or vision, it should be received as something personal. I am not of the opinion that everything I see in my mind's eye at night is a guaranteed supernatural message from above for the masses to hear. As a prophet, Daniel was gifted with an ability to receive divine messages, but he knew it was necessary to discern the message first and not make it immediately known to the public. It is written about his experience that it was so troubling, he kept it to himself.

At this point the revelation ended. As for me, Daniel, my thoughts were greatly alarming me and my face grew pale, but I kept the matter to myself."
Daniel 7:28

Daniel was set apart and gifted to receive this kind of communication from The Spirit. And because of this gift, he was entrusted with a troubling message that he could hold and know what to do with.

In the 2020 US presidential election, many claimed God had told them in a vision that Donald J. Trump would be reelected president of the United States. I found it fascinating to watch many of them try to explain why their candidate lost the election when God had spoken so clearly prior to that second Tuesday in November.. As I understand them, visions are usually very personal experiences. And since they are so personal, it makes sense to keep them quiet. What was the value of making those visions of Trump publicly known? Why did these preachers and pastors feel the need to make a prediction that would not come true? Why run the risk of losing credibility by making a false claim? I believe this was why Daniel kept quiet. He was entrusted with an enormous message. It would take time to sort out such a weighty vision.

Prophetic visions have much value to the person receiving them. They are not a license or means for Christian fortune telling. I like to think of them as intimate gifts from The Lover of My Soul.

2. Write the vision down.

This seems a bit obvious, but it is very important to have a record of what is being received, especially if you receive dreams and visions regularly. Keeping a record helps me discern what is being conveyed to my heart. Writing lets me see if a pattern emerges, even though it may not be relevant in the immediate circumstances.

My bias in this matter comes from my experience with seeing dreams and visions and holding onto them privately. Some who discern these types of prophetic messages believe they are given to be passed on to someone who needs to hear them. I don't swim in that water. Every dream and vision I have seen over the years has been given to me and for me alone to consider. After receiving each of them, I write them down so I can refer to them when circumstances begin to become contradictory or confusing. I believe a dream or vision is a means of producing a picture that I can clearly see in my mind in order to anchor my faith as it is being called upon to expand.

An advantage I have here is that I am a writer and journaling comes naturally to me. I learned journaling when I was a freshman in college and have practiced it ever since. I say this because writing is difficult for many. Journaling has an ought to element to it. Many think they ought to do it out of compulsion. But in the case of seeing a vision, it's vital to jot it down in some form. I have had enough of them to know to take them seriously enough to put them on paper.

3. Share it with a trusted soul.

This can be the most difficult, especially if you don't have a friend whose faith flourishes in this arena. The value of this step is to garner understanding, not approval. We all need people in our lives who can bear witness to what is happening to us and in us. Whether it is grief, loss, sorrow, or celebration, not having to walk alone is a special gift.

I have a few of these trustworthy friends, but one in particular, whom I refer to as The Man of God, is one of the first I rely on for insight. He has been distinct in how he listens to my vision and reflects on what he takes from it. And he was the first one I went to with this most major vision when I received it in 2003.

Your faith requires
A vast language
Equal to the size
Of the wide-open expanse
Of the new life
You are discovering

Faith needs
An ever expanding
Language
If it intends
To represent
The impossible

Faith seeks
Words
That look
And sound
Like her

A person's faith
Enlarges
When their vernacular
Follows suit

As your faith
Burgeons
So will the words
You use
To describe it

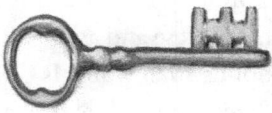

CHAPTER 2

FAITH AND THE USE OF METAPHOR

The importance of metaphor

We would not have an understanding of God without the implementation of metaphor. Repeatedly, the words of scripture include comparisons using this literary device. While this is not an exhaustive list, here are a few word pictures from both the Old and New Testaments:

- God is my rock
  – 2 Samuel 22:3
- God is my shield
  – Psalm 18:2
- God is the King of all the earth
  – Psalm 47:7
- God is spirit
  – John 4:24
- God is the builder of everything.
  – Hebrews 3:4
- God is a consuming fire
  – Hebrews 12:29
- God is light
  – 1 John 1:5

Each one of these is like an old Polaroid snapshot; it is worth a thousand words. They are useful comparisons for me, due to the impossibility of a finite mind like mine comprehending The Infinite Being. How does one describe The Almighty? With metaphor, of course.

The beauty of metaphor is in the imagination it invokes. When I say "something is like . . ." I'm honoring you and trusting you to add your perspective. I could take each one of these and ask, "Why this word? Why is God like a rock? Why did the author use that word? Is God hardheaded? Or solid?"

And why is God considered like a shield or a builder or a consuming fire? These words are full of invitation to explore the nature of The One who shields, builds, and burns.

Extend this use of comparison to the ways Jesus tried to convey the nature of the Kingdom from which he came. When my kids were very young, they both loved to hear stories from me. When they would ask a difficult question, I often resorted to telling a story as the answer. One question I recall was, "Dad, what's it like to be a grown-up?" I knew I had to come up with an answer a child could understand and not describe it from an adult's point of view. So, I took their young minds into consideration and said, "It's a little like being a kid. You still get to play and have fun, but you have to do lots more chores and nobody tucks you into bed or reads to you at night. You have to do that yourself." Then the child-like questions came. "Are you sad that nobody reads to you?" or "Do grown-ups have a bedtime?" Even though they could not comprehend fully what it was like to be a grown-up, they trusted me to be close enough to hold them. I always had fun interacting with my kids in this way.

Metaphor to Convey an Idea

As a creative and intuitive person, I am drawn to the ways we are shown in the Gospel accounts of how Jesus chose to teach and convey his message of the Kingdom of Heaven. He used stories, parables, and metaphors to compare what his reality looks and feels like in contrast to the physical life he was living on earth.

The Judge and The Widow

One story that Jesus told that had a significant influence on me in my developing years is recorded in the Gospel of Luke, beginning in Chapter 18, verses 1 through 8. Jesus wanted to convey the essence of what prayer is like, so He chose to tell a parable. He began by describing the court of a mean and heartless judge. I imagine he chose this illustration because his listeners likely related, especially living in a day where there was little legal recourse or appeal like we know today. Folks in his audience may have had a family member or friend stand before the very same type of judge. So, he seeks to build a connection of understanding right from the start.

The next character he introduces is a widow. Again, quite likely she was a person many people could fashion an image of. Could it be he was referring to an actual woman in that town, not a hypothetical figure? He describes her as persistent because she kept appearing before this unwelcoming judge, asking him to grant her justice against her adversary.

As time went by, the judge put her off and refused to make a ruling in her case. But he began to foresee unfavorable consequences. Jesus described the inner dialogue in which the judge was engaging. He said to himself, "If I don't do something soon, this woman might harm me!"

I find this such an interesting comparison. Jesus introduces an idea of prayer by using a familiar scenario. He allows for a story with details that could be misconstrued or misunderstood. As a storyteller, I know how a listener can grab ahold of a detail, get stuck on it, and not be able to get past it. I get responses like, "So what you're saying is . . .?!?" No, I'm not saying that. Stay with me. The point of the story is mixed in with all the minor details of the parable. This is the value of a parable. It's an invitation to listen and pay attention. Thus, Jesus said, "Whoever has ears to hear, let him hear."

The Point of the Metaphor

The point wasn't about the uncaring justice nor the grudge-bearing woman who might take revenge on him. Nor do I think the point was about how to get what you want from prayer by how many times you ask to the point of being a pest. I believe the crux was in his last statement:

> *"However, when the Son of Man comes, will he find faith on the earth?"*
> Luke 18:8

It is easy to approach this parable as a how-to, cause-and-effect equation. I was taught that this passage shows me how I should pray to get what I want. The usual conclusion was to be persistent in my request, ask over and over and over again, and eventually, I will be heard and get my answer. From my upbringing, I can see how this conclusion would be reached, but it eventually breaks down if I stay with it long enough.

What is Jesus hoping to convey? What did he hope his followers would take away from this moment? Was he saying his Father in heaven would give in after enough complaints? Was he telling them to be as bitchy as possible and hold out until they break him down? Again, I have seen how this might make sense to some, but I think there is far more to take away here—a far more beautiful and intimate picture.

I reflect on Jesus' closing question. "Will he find faith?" This takes precedence over all the other elements in the story. Faith is the one quality he will be looking for when he returns for his Bride. Everything in the parable now becomes about faith, and I need to see it through those lenses. This changes how I read the parable.

The chapter opens with this introduction:

> *Then Jesus told his disciples a parable to show them they should always pray and not give up.*
>
> Luke 18:1

Instead of diligently studying the text in order to come out with a demonstrable checklist, I get to consider how my faith is going to thrive, but that's not how I was taught. Here's how I was once shown to see it:

1. I am to come to My Father in prayer.
2. I bring my request to him persistently.
3. The more I ask, the better chance I have of getting my desired answer.

The problem with this method is that I can do all this, and faith is not required. That is why I believe Jesus finished the story with the question, "Will He find faith?" Here's how I now understand what faith is.

The Essence of Faith

For purposes of this discussion, and to help you understand where I am going, we need a definition of faith. I never ask my reader to agree with me, but it is important that I am clear in what I am saying. To a communicator, misunderstanding is a painful outcome of the failed attempt to communicate. Therefore, I aim for clarity, not agreement.

The most reasonable place to begin is Hebrews 11, the chapter that is all about the faith woven throughout history and recorded in the Old Testament.

Now faith is confidence in what we hope for and assurance about what we do not see. This is what the ancients were commended for.

Hebrews 11:1

Confidence and Assurance

The first two words I contemplate are confidence and assurance.

Wherever faith is found, there will also be a confidence attached to it—specifically, confidence in what we hope for.

Faith doesn't necessarily need to be a spiritual thing. I can have faith in the airline industry because I have confidence that the plane will get me to my destination. It has a good and trustworthy track record of getting lots of people from point A to point B, so I buy a ticket and board a jet with a sense of confidence.

Next is the word assurance. How does this play into the spirit of faith? The author of Hebrews explains that faith makes room for the unseen; therefore, one who holds faith exudes a sense of assurance that what cannot be seen can become an experienced reality.

Taking the parable of Jesus about the judge and widow, how does it change the story when I factor in confidence and assurance? With these two lenses, it becomes less about the mechanics and more about the longing of the heart. Confidence in the request. Confidence in the one I am approaching and appealing to. Assurance that what I need will be taken seriously and the favorable answer will come to pass.

And where does this confidence and assurance originate?

For the airline industry, where does my confidence lie? It comes from reputation and experience. My very first flight was on a Pan Am 747 jet when I was nine years old. I was so scared at the sheer size of this aircraft, but my young nerves calmed down once we were in the air, and it was apparent it wasn't going to crash. Now, as an adult, I regularly get on board without thought or hesitation because I have faith that the plane will do what it was designed to do.

In the same way, my assurance in getting to where I want to go is secure even though I haven't arrived yet. I take my past experience along with the experience of countless other travelers and conclude that I will get to where I haven't been yet.

So now I can take the parable and apply the same sense of confidence and assurance to my requests. The first time I am in need and decide to ask The Divine Judge for help in prayer might feel like the nine-year-old boy and his maiden voyage on a jet plane. I'm understandably unsure, but I will move forward anyway. I don't have to keep count of the number of times I ask and question whether I've asked enough. I can press in with confidence and assurance that The Judge is trustworthy and true. If a favorable outcome can happen between a heartless judge and a nagging widow, how much more via faith in One Who is Gracious?

When Metaphor Isn't Necessary

Jesus could have given a different teaching on the lesson of how to pray and not give up. He could have given a very modern, Western description with three points and two illustrations for each one. He could have supernaturally produced handouts with these three points and granted everyone the power to read them. He could have outlined the three steps to successful prayer, but he didn't.

Facts, Data, and Information.

Instead, he used a parable, a type of metaphor that employs descriptive mental imagery in the storytelling and requires imagination on the part of the hearer to grasp its meaning. He didn't outline facts and statements. And of course, there is nothing wrong with facts and statements. They are helpful in communicating specifics when the conclusion of the message is factual. Take for example, emailing your team regarding someone's question about what the staff meeting is going to be about and what time everyone should show up. It's easiest to say we are talking about the new policy change regarding employee compensation, and we will get started at 10:00 a.m. There is little need for nuance or cleverness. Imagine getting an email like this:

> *There once was a flock of geese that were all flying south together in formation, and a few disgruntled geese saw that not everyone was taking their turn leading out front but expected the same grain at the end of the day as those who did the hard work. The geese will discuss this disagreement when all geese land in the same field.*

This metaphor is not helpful in informing the staff of the time and topic. To just say, "We're discussing employee compensation at ten this morning" is adequate. But Jesus was not inviting his followers to a meeting but to contemplate a deep and complex mystery of prayer. Since prayer is magnificent and vast, he chose to couch it in the language of metaphor. Sometimes mystery is best explained with another mystery. Therefore, he told a story about an unconcerned judge and persistent widow and gave our imagination permission to explore the metaphor.

———————————

I don't seek
To inspire
Through my writing
I'm only trying
To open a window
And let in
A little fresh air
For us all to breathe
A little easier

If my faith

Constantly needs

Defending

Shouldn't I

Be concerned?

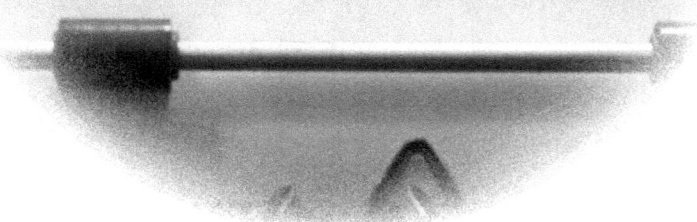

CHAPTER 3

BIAS WITHIN THE METAPHOR

Our Past Shapes How We See

From my bent, I could argue that there is no more significant metaphor in the New Testament than that of God as Father. As a dad, I have a special appeal when it comes to considering the nature and character of The One Who Loves Me through my firsthand experience as a father of raising two (now adult) children. I am drawn into this imagery that is deeply rooted in the storytelling of Jesus. I was fortunate to have been raised by a warm, thoughtful, witty, and wise father. He's been gone for nineteen years now, but I see his influence all over me. Even though he wasn't a writer, his words are in mine now as I write. It is not difficult for my faith to thrive within this metaphor. I trusted my dad and looked to him for all kinds of advice. He was a good teacher and showed me how to use power tools, probably at too young an age and certainly to the chagrin of my mother. But he believed in me and let me take risks without overprotecting me.

With this example, God as Father makes sense to me, but not everyone is as fortunate. If you grew up with an absent father, or an abusive one, or one who was nonplussed and disinterested in your life, this experience will cloud your understanding of this metaphor. For you, the very thought of a father is unfavorable and maybe even repulsive. If your father was an alcoholic and unpredictable, you are not to blame if you feel like God is like the person who raised you.

This doesn't negate the metaphor, but it does mean there will be challenges for you to thrive within it. The story of the prodigal son reveals this.

Two Boys. Same Dad. Different Behaviors.

Many are familiar with this story in the eighteenth chapter of the book of Luke about a son who squanders his father's inheritance, eventually hits rock bottom, and comes back home to seek care from his father. But let's look at it from the perception of the father by the prodigal son and his older brother. How did these two boys view their dad? They had different points of view of him, both from within whatever experiences they were raised.

We can infer that their father was a good person, but that knowledge did not endear the two sons to see him as he was. One was reckless and given to lust. The other was bound to duty and obligation. Both had the same dad, and both had a distinct take on him and acted accordingly.

The younger son saw his father as someone to take advantage of. The older saw him as weak and foolish.

The younger son acted consistently from his attitude toward his father and took advantage of him. The older stayed put but grew angry and resentful.

The younger son became desperate and saw his father as a viable option to escape his desperation. The older son grew jealous and despised his brother and father.

Both boys had misperceptions about their father. Yet the father was patient with both, knowing they would not change their minds until they were at a place where a change of mind made sense to them.

My Own Bias

Graham Cooke says, "We all come to faith on a fraction of the truth," meaning we don't have the full picture yet of the One Who Loves Us Best. The summer after I graduated high school and right before going to college, I decided that I would get my life right with The Man Upstairs. But it was mostly out of fear of going to hell. My hell/fire/brimstone upbringing made hell the most important thing on my teenage mind. And since I didn't want to go there, I believed I should straighten up, fly right, and do what The Man Upstairs said. So, I prayed a simple prayer of faith, and my life changed immediately.

Mine was the tradition of the Southern Baptist denomination. For those unfamiliar with this expression of Christianity, this community is synonymous with a high view and reverence for the truth and validity of the Bible. It was a given to believe that scripture was the inerrant and infallible Word of God and contained all the instruction one needed to live the way God intended his people to live. It was rarely questioned in my circles of association.

Bias against the Bible

When I was very young and just learning to read, I remember reading from the family Bible that stayed out on the coffee table. It was a thick, leather-bound text written in the King James version. It had color lithographs of famous paintings situated between the Old and New Testaments. My parents would let me take a turn reading a passage as I got more and more comfortable with big words. I specifically recall being encouraged to sound out *King Nebuchadnezzar* as we read from the book of Daniel. Little me would stumble through the phonetics, "NEB-yoo-CHAD-nezzzzer." Mom and Dad didn't correct me but took delight in watching me learn.

As a youth, I had plenty of church attendance to make me familiar with the Bible, but more accurately, familiar with the way angry men screamed and shouted their interpretation of it. In those days, it was normal for a preacher to yell at the congregation with calls of shame and contempt about how everyone should tithe more, witness more, and be at more meetings. But given my isolated environment, I had no other reason to think that things could ever be different. It was generally an unwritten assumption that the reason you went to church was to get your weekly beating for being such a wretched soul. I got beaten at school. Why would I expect church to be any different?

I never took the Bible seriously until I went to college. My mom gave me a black, cloth-bound Bible, also a King James. It was my first foray into discovering for myself what this tradition was all about. When I entered the university, I found a collegiate ministry, also of Southern Baptist flavor, to get involved in. I met some great friends during those five years. I'm still connected with some of them more than forty years later.

We don't know what we don't know. It's not wise to try to answer questions for others that they aren't asking. This book is a retelling of how I experienced my own apocalypse. I use this word not in a doomsday sense. This misappropriated word literally means to take the lid off. It is most often used to refer to the end of days and life as we know it. And this is not entirely inaccurate. Through the tutelage of the Holy Spirit, the lid was taken off my life so I could see inside and identify how my past influences had shaped an unhelpful paradigm. In the chapters ahead, I will describe this process that led to the end of a restrictive life of faith as I once knew it.

Learn the Rules

In the beginning of my newly discovered faith, I was strongly encouraged to make the Bible a daily part of my life. Never had I even considered reading it regularly on my own outside of Sunday mornings. My new friends all seemed to make time every day to read the Bible. They called it a quiet time. I thought it sounded like something that should happen at daycare, not in college. I joined in anyway. I would grab my black, cloth-bound King James Bible and a little notebook and pen and go downstairs to a study lounge in the basement of my college dormitory. Ever since I was a young child, I was a morning person. This served me well in those early quiet times. There was not a soul stirring at 6:30 in the morning, so I had my pick of the study booths. In the solitude of that space, my budding young faith took root. I'm ever grateful for learning that practice.

I learned quickly that the Bible was not a book to be read like a novel. I thought it was too confusing and disjointed and didn't make sense. My peers showed me a little method for approaching these scriptures that I wanted to understand but lacked the education and knowledge to do so.

I was taught to use a little acronym called SPACE whenever I read the Bible. This five-letter word stood for five questions I was to ask myself as I studied the text:

Is there a:
- Sin to confess?
- Promise to keep?
- Attitude to change?
- Command to obey?
- Example to follow?

Anytime I went into my basement hideaway, I was encouraged to bring a notebook and pen along with my Bible and record the answers to these questions. And as a young college freshman of eighteen, this was a reasonable starting point congruent with what I had understood about what it meant to have faith in God.

Little did I know that another bias was silently being formed.

Bias against God

The timbre of the church teaching of the day was that my natural tendency was to drift away from my new-found faith and into a life of sin. I was taught to believe that I was a bad kid who was constantly sinful and would continually be prone to do the wrong thing and thus always in need of constant correction. The little acronym was built on this assumption; therefore, I learned how to read the Bible by looking for all the things I was doing wrong. I would not say this methodology was incorrect or bad. I now label it as incomplete. However, the Holy Spirit has a way of taking something incomplete and nudging me forward to new ways to consider and be inspired by his story throughout the generations.

All I knew of myself was what my elders told me, which was mainly to sit down and shut up. School felt like a type of prison, and I was locked up for being myself. I was a clever kid, quick with wit, and loved to make people laugh. In my senior year, I was voted class clown and had a long list of pranks to prove I deserved the award. One time in English class, I had a severe nosebleed. It was profuse and dripping on my desk. I asked my teacher if I could go to the bathroom, and she told me no and to stay seated. Another classmate spoke up on my behalf and urged the teacher to let me go take care of it. I remember the look of horror on her face when she saw it really was blood and that I wasn't faking it. She assumed I had broken open a red ink pen and was looking for a way to skip class. She recalled that story to me every time I saw her for years after I graduated. I was such a jokester, she figured I was up to my usual chicanery.

To always be held in suspicion as a child by adults didn't create any kind of trust on my part. Consequently, I was afraid of adults. What other conclusion would I reach if I was told to sit down and be quiet or else face a beating? It diminished my self-concept and tarnished my sense of worth.

All these past and very personal stories influenced the reason why I thought the Bible was given to us. The primary metaphor for the way I viewed the Bible was as a lawbook. I assumed the sixty-six books of the Old and New Testaments were full of laws and rules to keep. The Bible's purpose was to point out my flaws and failures and reveal all the ways I was not living up to the standard written within.

In my developing faith, it was easy to embrace this blueprint because I felt I was a bad kid who always got in trouble at school. And now that I had decided to follow God, he must think the same about me. The predominant attitude toward me from my teachers and adults was negative. I was a troublemaker and needed to be kept in check and silenced. One teacher in particular emphasized this. On the first day of math class when I moved up to high school, he came straight over to my desk, wagged his finger in my face, and said, "I've heard about you, and you are not going to disrupt my classroom. If you think you can, then try me."

What did I do? Of course, I tested him. His challenge beckoned me to silently reply, "Game on." And I paid a price during the next three years of high school for taking that dare.

Keep in mind that I grew up in a time period and a part of the country where corporal punishment was actively in use in public schools. For those uninformed, that means physical beatings with a wooden paddle on the buttocks. It was a humiliating yet acceptable practice at that time. But to me, it eventually became a badge of honor. After a whipping, before the next class began, I would go into the bathroom to survey the damage. Bright red welts showed up on my butt cheeks, and occasionally visible bruising from broken blood vessels that would look worse the next day. Other boys thought I was a war hero for not sucking up to the teacher and taking the punishment like a man.

He Will Beat the Hell Out of Me.

Now that I had discovered faith in God, why would he think of me or treat me any differently? I just assumed he was going to act like my teacher and proceed to beat the sin and hell out of me.

There were times I had no idea what I had done wrong, and no explanation was given for the spanking. I think I looked at the teacher wrong one morning and his face turned red with rage. He grabbed me by the arm, forced me out into the hallway, and pushed me up against the lockers. I put out my hands to lean against the metal doors and took five loud swats to my ass. Nothing was said. I just went back to my seat and sat down gingerly on my stinging butt.

The metaphor of God I held was directly shaped by this abusive experience. Even though God was supposed to be my father, I had different lenses obscuring my view of who I had yet to be introduced to.

My bias was reinforced.

In my eighteen-year-old mind, I saw God as the one in charge, and I had no say or recourse in any matter. Just like my teachers, I assumed he would need to beat out of me all the wrongs and behaviors of which he didn't approve. He wouldn't even have to tell me what I did wrong. He would just make me read my Bible longer and find more SPACE to deal with.

It took the concerted effort of counseling for me as a midlife adult to go back to those younger days of mistreatment and reconnect with the pain inflicted by these coldhearted men. Such is the case when trying to work out the wounding that is rooted in the body of anyone who has faced traumatic events or, even worse, repeated traumatic patterns. I refer to my therapist as Keyholder because that's what she was for me.

Let me explain what I mean by Keyholder.

I can lock most of the doors in my house and truck without a key, but I can't open them back up without one. I use this metaphor to remind me that even though I may not have planned to be in a particular unfavorable predicament, I will certainly need some help getting out of it. And a Keyholder is a person in my life who holds the insight, discernment, and wisdom to assist me in unlocking the past that has bound me within abuse and prevented me from moving toward a life of fullness and freedom.

During a therapy session, Keyholder asked me a random question, and in my answer, I included a story about how I was regularly spanked during my high school years. She stopped me immediately and asked urgently, "Wait. Can you say that part again?" I told her about the time I received five swats of a paddle for talking out of line in class.

Puzzled, she asked me if this was a normal occurrence, to which I replied in the affirmative. I told her I received these swats on a regular basis. She gently corrected me and said, "Kevin, what you just described are not swats. These were beatings. You were repeatedly beaten, not disciplined. She asked one more revealing question: "Can you see this as abuse?" I said, "No. I guess I thought it was just high school."

This interaction with Keyholder opened a massive closet with skeletons of pain and mistreatment toward me by other teachers and school authority figures. What I thought was normal, Keyholder redefined it for me as abnormal and damaging. Little did I know what was coming next. I had to come to terms with how this upbringing colored my view of The Author of My Faith.

I didn't realize that the fraction of the truth I had embraced at the beginning was not the full picture. And it was subject to change through the invitation of The Wild Goose.

Interesting that
The son of man
Gave us no teaching
Or instruction
On what to do
With unanswered prayer

To do so
Would imply
That it's okay
For me
To settle
For nothing

CHAPTER 4

FIRE IN THE BONES

Unknowingly, how I viewed my Creator and the Bible was strongly tainted by the hurts in my past. Instead of seeing God as a gracious Heavenly Father, I saw him as an authority figure who didn't really like me, but I had to do what he said or else. He thought I was a pest and a nuisance who interrupted classrooms and needed to be constantly told to sit down and shut up. His Bible was his rulebook, given to keep me in line, so if I wanted to stay out of trouble, I had better read it and know what it says.

Dan Allender, a noted author about sexual abuse and shame, says the only thing we can't see of ourself is our face. We can only see a reflection of it. This is one reason that healing of our past perception and perspective needs to take place within a community of trusted souls who understand what you are going through. And they can read it on our face. They can see if what we are saying matches up with our body language. It will soon be self-evident if the two are incongruent and mismatched. Like when I told Keyholder that I thought getting beaten at school was normal—she assured me it wasn't and invited me to hear her describe my face. I was the man sitting in her office telling the facts of a story of abuse who couldn't hide the pain revealed in his eyes. That's why it is so important for restoration to take place among the gifted healers.

The language of devotion to God will be congruent with the actions from the same source. There was a time when I would have said I was wholly devoted to God, but my emotions and body language would not have supported that statement. A person of faith will continually be bringing these two aspects of their life in line.

It wasn't an overnight makeover. It took many months of reenvisioning what was possible in what I wanted my future with My Maker to look like.

Acknowledging the Fire

How did I know I had an incomplete, limiting bias against My Maker? How does a person become aware if they are missing a piece or two from their picture?

My past experiences and influences skewed my understanding of The Author of My Faith. I had a concept of father, even of what a good father could be, but it was misapplied because of abusive figures along the way. Unknowingly, I embraced My Father in heaven as a controlling authority figure of whom I was deeply terrified. Thankfully, that image has sprouted and blossomed into a more beautiful understanding of The One Who Loves Me Most.

If, as you are reading this, you feel a tug that is pulling you into considering my words, it's likely from the gentleness of The Comforter inviting you to sit and listen together. I accept that I am biased in my story, and what I write on these pages is just that. It's my story of how I discovered faith as a teenager and the process of continually being guided into a place where that young faith can mature and thrive. I've written enough over the years to know that the words of my story can be upsetting to one and soothing to another. My goal is not to create unanimity. I'm writing because of the compulsion to do so. The prophet Jeremiah had the same feeling:

> But if I say, "I will not mention his word or speak anymore in his name," his word is in my heart like a fire, a fire shut up in my bones. I am weary of holding it in; indeed, I cannot.
>
> Jeremiah 20:9

I personally identify with this metaphor of fire in the bones. There have been times when I have felt compelled to write, and I'm not entirely sure why. When my late wife first discovered that she had ovarian cancer, my first impulse after her surgery was to go home and write about it. I immediately wanted to tell her story. I didn't want to hide it or hold it in. I didn't want to try and keep it a secret. There was something in me that needed to let it out. And I needed to be true to that.

I believe this sense of fire is one of the many ways The Still Small Voice gets my attention as it moves within me. It is highly intuitive and harmonious with how I naturally tune into my inner and outer world. There are times when I look at someone and feel they are troubled. I have learned that is my cue to slow down and pay attention to what I just picked up. It may be there for me to see if this person needs help or a positive word or just a pleasant smile. It may be for nothing more than for me to tune into a broader perspective than getting caught up in the troubles of my own little world. This awareness can lead to a resetting of my focus and move me away from worry into peace.

The fire in the bones was one of the first metaphors from which I started gleaning early in my faith. It was the prompting that convinced me to take faith seriously on June 20, 1981. For a year and a half prior, I carried an unsettling sense that I was not right with My Maker and needed to give my full attention to this fire shut up in my bones. I recall many late nights in bed, staring up at the ceiling, with the burning feeling inside me to go all in and make faith in My Maker my highest priority. And I did. And I've been on an amazing path since then.

Dousing the Fire

But somewhere along the way, my focus on The Still Small Voice switched to an emphasis on written text. I eagerly immersed myself in the study of the text but found I was less likely to trust The Still Small Voice because of how I was taught. There were some who led me to believe that the text was all I needed to pay attention to and every answer I needed was written within its pages. I should never trust what could be confused as a feeling or impulse and only stick to the words of the text. I was taught to distrust these feelings since they are susceptible to the whims of my untrustworthy heart.

I bought into this idea for several years until the fire in my bones started getting hot. I had to confront the juxtaposition of the coolness of the faith heritage that had shaped me with the new warmth I was experiencing within. I wasn't seeing new and inspiring faith in the lives of those who led me and the communities that housed limiting beliefs. I could tell my faith was not going to thrive there. So I decided to trust The Still Small Voice again and embark on a new path.

My first step was to leave the professional vocational ministry I had been involved in for eighteen years. Ministry was my career path. I assumed I would do this for the rest of my days and then retire and do something retired pastors do, like write or play golf. But my faith had been attached to a means of earning a living, and I was growing increasingly uncomfortable with this exchange. Many are gifted and talented to express their faith in the service of the office of pastor. I finally accepted that I am not one of them.

It didn't take long before my decision got tested, leaving me to wonder if I had made a huge mistake. Within a month after leaving my ministry position, my wife lost her job, and my dad passed away. I wondered, "Is this the way it's supposed to go?" I started second guessing myself. Were my leaders right? Had I trusted my feelings and emotions and taken my eyes off the instruction of the written text?

As I look back now, I can see from experience that any future step of faith I take will be tested. It's the natural way The Fire burns within me. And I have learned to expect no less. I had left the ministry to find my faith again, but nothing was going as planned. I never expected it would be so difficult. But then again, faith is about being sure of what I hope for and certain of what I can't see. I hoped for a more vibrant faith, and I certainly couldn't see it. It would take a while before I could see that I had made the right choice to leave the old behind in hopes of a better future.

The fire shut up in my bones led me to where I am today. And it took a long time to trust it. But it's compelling me to write about my experience from my unique vantage point. I compare it to the metaphor of witnessing a car collision at a busy intersection. There may be multiple eyewitnesses on all four corners of the scene, and each might give a slightly different account of what they saw regarding the exact same event. Living a life of faith is a little like that. Because of different vantage points, we should expect to gather a fuller picture than if we just listened to one voice who considers himself an expert on auto crashes. This is how I understand The Ancient Text. Sixty-six books hold the accounts of people who held onto the red thread of faith woven through history. Each writer will lend their observation of what they witnessed from The Author of Faith.

And I am no different in writing what I have seen in my brief time here on the planet. I am one voice among billions who have lived and seen a story. And I choose to chime in from the place I stand and add my lyrics to the Divine Composition played out among humanity.

When learning to hear
The voice
Of your maker
Find the kindest voice
In your head
And follow
That one

I defend

That which is weak

And vulnerable

Those are not words

I associate

With the strength

Of faith

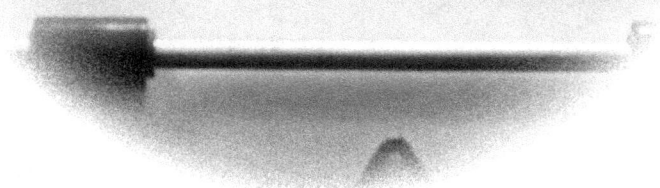

CHAPTER 5

THE ADVOCATE

Metaphors abound when it comes to describing the personality and work of the one known in scripture as the Holy Spirit. I have my favorites and even make up a few for my own personal enjoyment. But my first introduction to The One Who Pursues My Heart would be as The Hound of Heaven. The phrase "The Hound of Heaven" was coined by poet Francis Thompson in 1893. He likened this person of the Godhead to a purebred hunting dog bent on tracking down the desired prize of the hunt. The hound will stop at nothing until the prey has become exhausted from the chase and is left with no recourse other than surrender.

This feels like the exact way I came to discover faith in the summer of 1981. I had been willfully ignoring the invitation to embrace faith for a year and a half. But there were circumstances that served notice that The Hound of Heaven was hot on my trail. I was involved in a severe car accident as a senior in high school that could have easily ended my life had the car flipped over, but instead it only skidded off the wet road and down an embankment. For some reason, the car slid down the slope, and the left rear quarter panel slammed into a large tree. All four of us crawled out of the wreckage and walked up the hill to flag down help. No one was injured, but the car was totaled. Even as a seventeen-year-old kid, this gave me a sense of my mortality. I reviewed the scenario over and over in my head. "I could be dead," I thought, "but I'm not. Why is that?" I'm not sure it was a sense of destiny that arrested my attention, but I did wonder why I was still alive. This question, coupled with the sound of the Hound of Heaven on my heels, led me to eventually relent and allow myself to be overcome like a fearful rabbit running from an incessant beagle.

The Hound of Heaven is just one of many metaphors to describe the person known as The Spirit. This is the beauty of metaphor. The infinite complexity of The Divine is multifaceted, much like a diamond. It gleams and glimmers with every ray of light and shift of movement. I think it's helpful to look at what Jesus had to say about His powerful coworker and next of kin. This is not an exhaustive study of the role and work of The Spirit of Kindness. But I want to highlight a few descriptions that I feel are important.

The apostle John records his recollection of Jesus' last days. He tells us his story of the events beginning in chapters 13 through 16 of his gospel.

> *It was just before the Passover Festival. Jesus knew that the hour had come for him to leave this world and go to the Father.*
>
> John 13:1

In this recorded exchange, Jesus had been saying some very hard things for his followers to hear. He spoke of persecution, suffering, and eventual death that would come about because of him and his teachings. In light of this, it was understandable that those who were looking to Jesus for guidance and support were beginning to feel uncertain and fearful. He knew this and chose to address it. He spoke the words that would bring comfort and engage the faith of those who believed in him.

I've witnessed death up close a few times. I watched my wife pass at age sixty and, eight months later, sat with my mom as she left us at the age of eighty-five. The process of dying brings about conflicting emotions, especially if there is significant pain and suffering involved. For a loved one to die suddenly is very painful, but to watch a person go through a sustained decline of body and mind is akin to torture. The survivors want their loved one to not be in pain, all the while managing their own distress of envisioning the inevitable loss of their dear dying soul.

The one who is near death also carries their own grief. They know they are the cause of the pain of everyone surrounding their deathbed. And they also have a sense of reality the survivors don't have. The authors of the book Final Gifts term this "the near-death experience." Those in this state often have an overwhelming concern for the well-being of those they are leaving behind. They want to know that their loved ones will be taken care of.

They want to get their affairs in order, so they write a will and make sure their death isn't a burden on anyone. This is a normal part of dying. Even my mom, before she died, told me, "Take good care of my grandchildren." We instinctively do whatever it takes to ensure a safe transition when shaking off the mortal coil.

I believe Jesus was no different. He knew his life was close to completion and death was imminent. It was clear that his followers were grieving because he was their teacher, saying upsetting words that they didn't want to hear. He knew what was playing out in their bodies. He could read it in them, and he knew what they would need. They would need an advocate, someone who would represent them on his behalf and who could do more for them than he could in bodily form as flesh and blood.

The Role of the Advocate

Jesus knew of certain unfavorable things to come that his followers did not. He knew he would have to go to the cross to suffer and die for them, but he also knew it was not hopeless, despite what they perceived. I see this scene as a way wherein Jesus is getting his affairs in order as he prepares for his death and departure from the ones he loves. He introduces a new person in his story: one known as The Advocate. This person will come and take his place and continue the work with his followers that he began.

> But very truly I tell you, it is for your good that I am going away. Unless I go away, The Advocate will not come to you; but if I go, I will send him to you.

> John 16:7

I can imagine these were hard and puzzling words to understand. Everything that had been happening was brand new. No person had ever performed the kinds of miracles that Jesus did. A touch of his garment would release healing power. And beyond the healings and restorations, there was the way he treated people. He spoke of forgiveness and kindness unlike any other teacher. He treated women in the most compassionate way, especially women who would be considered "fallen." I'm sure every person who was endeared to Jesus thought, "Who is this man? Who else can do the things he does?" I can also imagine a second thought followed:

"I don't want to lose this man. He means everything to me."

One normal reaction in the grief process is panic. Impending loss can whip the nervous system into a frenzy. And loss because of death is permanent; it can lead to deep despair. And Jesus knows all of this. He is not caught off guard or found unaware. He has kept the grief of his followers in mind as he sets his affairs in order.

A Better Judge.

Jesus describes in more detail The Advocate who will represent him after he departs from his followers' physical presence. He goes so far as to tell them that The Advocate will do a better job of teaching them what they need to know and providing a better source of comfort than he could in physical form. He tries to help them understand how life will be better once The Advocate comes and takes over the role that Jesus began.

> *When he comes, he will prove the world to be in the wrong about sin and righteousness and judgment.*
>
> John 16:8

Proving what was right and who was wrong had long been the job of the Pharisees. They were seen as the rule keepers. They made the decisions about judgment. Their leaders would ask him questions like this:

> *"Rabbi, whose fault was it that this man was born blind?"*
>
> John 9:2

A Pharisee always wanted to get to the bottom of the problem and relied on the rule of law to secure the right answer. The movement of Pharisaical thought led them to consider themselves the experts in the laws of God. They put strong emphasis on interpreting the Mosaic law. So when Jesus appeared, he posed an immediate threat to their history of authority by how he spoke and how the common person received him.

Jesus' followers lived with personal experience of this thought regime. You can see it in the stories Jesus tells. You can see who had the most trouble with him. He was preparing them to be ready for a brand-new way of life, liberated from wrong and partial judgments. Right and wrong would no longer be decided by a group of men. The Advocate would be given that duty, and they would be so much better off under this new leadership.

Of Sin

As Jesus was pointing to a better future, he was giving hints to what this new life would look like for his followers. Up to then, sin was defined by a law. To break that law was considered sinful. All violations of the law required punishment, and the Pharisees held this title of judge and jury.

> *In regards about sin, because people do not believe in me.*
>
> John 16:9

This new representative would be the one to point out what sin is, because the law was just about to be fulfilled and become obsolete. So, without a law, who gets to decide what sin is? The Advocate would. In the coming era, sin would be tied to unbelief, not rule-breaking. And who knows the heart of a person except the spirit of that person? Motive and belief come into play as factors in determining what sin is. Under the rule of law, it's external and straightforward. But with The Advocate, it's all about belief. And a counsel of men is not equipped to judge the hearts of those who claim Jesus as their Teacher.

Of Righteousness

To be righteous means to be in right standing before the law. The Pharisees got to make rulings on this, too. They were the ones who knew the law better than any other group of people; therefore, they decided who was righteous or not. The change away from this practice was another description of the role of The Advocate, who was soon to come and take over the work of Jesus.

> *About righteousness, because I am going to the Father, where you can see me no longer;*
>
> John 16:10

Jesus would be the full embodiment of righteousness as he went to be with his Father and represent his followers before him. There would no longer be a need for a law to decide this status. The Advocate would be commissioned to reassure all of who believed in Jesus that everything is as he said it would be. Even though they would not be able to physically see Jesus any longer, they would be given full assurance of the truth of everything he said and did from the Advocate.

Of Judgment

To pass judgment is to assess a situation where a decision needs to be made about who is at fault and what damages need to be paid. Judgment is very important to social order. Without sound judgment, injustice will run amok. But judgment can easily be overtaken by corrupt forces that further anything but justice. The Advocate would represent those who were judged and treated unfairly.

> *And about judgment, because the prince of this world now stands condemned.*
>
> John 16:15

I especially take note whenever Jesus makes use of a metaphor. The reference to the Prince of This World is especially instructive within his explanation of the soon-coming Advocate. Jesus was clear in explaining that he and his kingdom were not of this world. The difference his followers were seeing was due to the clash of these two domains. The Kingdom of the Earth, where his followers lived, was governed by its own Prince through the limitations of law. The Prince of This World was the direct reason judgment was necessary in the first place. This domination would soon come to an end once Jesus ascended to the cross in the final act that would bring condemnation to The Prince of This World and set the entire world free from the law.

Apart from faith, there was no way for Jesus' followers to have any idea of the revolutionary way of life he was explaining. His Father was doing something brand new that had never been seen before in the history of humanity. I imagine the questions.

"Who is this Advocate of which you speak?"

"What will he look like?"

"How will we find him?"

These are all very reasonable questions. History was about to change, and faith was the only way to understand it. There would no longer be laws to keep and judge. There would be a freely offered union with The Advocate who would make possible a free and unfettered access to The Father and render the confines of the law irrelevant. Jesus had this kind of personal union with his Father, and it would be the very same union made available by faith to his followers.

New Access

Here's a small illustration about access, but it works for me. When I was a teenager, the only available access to listen to music was the radio, a concert, or purchasing a recording. This was the norm, and I consumed my share of music through all three means. If The Rainbow Station KMOD 97.5 FM wasn't playing in my room, there would be a record album spinning on my turntable. I immersed myself in music as it was the language of my heart and soul.

As the years went by and technology changed, the access didn't really change; just the format did. Long-play records gave way to the eight-track tape, which then morphed into the more preferred cassette tape. Then came the digital compact disc. It was still a recording, but how the sound was captured was completely different. Trying to keep up with the technology was expensive. And decisions were made to jettison the LPs and tapes in favor of the latest improvement.

Not long after came the method of streaming music. The new digital technology allowed the signal to be sent through a computer or phone, where music can be enjoyed in a more efficient way. This transformation eliminated the need to purchase vinyl records, tapes, or CDs. The generation of ownership was giving way to the age of access.

It was a puzzling dilemma for me. Do I pay $9.99 a month to have unlimited access to any song imaginable but have nothing to show for it in the form of a library or collection? Or do I stick with purchasing music like I always did and not be exposed to new artists and songs that I would otherwise miss? I could see a clear generation gap growing as I watched my teenage kids quickly adopt their new value of access over ownership. Unlike me, they owned nothing, though music was just as important to them as it had been to me when I was their age. They didn't have the cluttered crates of old records and boxes of unlistened-to tapes and CDs to sort through like I did. So, I followed their lead and paid the subscription. I still have a very small collection of recordings I kept after painstakingly going through hundreds of past favorites that no longer held any value to me.

It's a simple metaphor, but through it, I can see how Jesus was describing something similar. The only way his followers knew about being right with God was by keeping the rules. And for the Pharisees, the more rules, the better. But The Advocate would come to do away with all that accumulation. Through the combined work of Jesus and The Advocate, open access to The Father and all the blessings of his kingdom would be made available. There would be far more to discover because of this free access than through the limitations of the law.

To New Wine

Up until the death of Jesus, access to God was limited. A priest was required to present himself through a series of sacrifices and rituals on behalf of the chosen people. It was not casual or informal. It was an extraordinary undertaking to even consider approaching The Almighty. It would even be dangerous if the priest did not follow the proper protocol. It was nothing to be taken lightly.

This would have been the predominant paradigm in the minds of the audience of Jesus. And it would have been a huge hurdle to overcome in their thoughts. Ingrained in them would have been a feeling of fear and apprehension whenever the notion of God came up. Even as this one named Jesus spoke to them about the unusual nature of the Kingdom of Heaven, the current idea of the religious rules and laws would have been firmly entrenched in their understanding.

This could be why he chose to use the metaphor of Advocate as he was introducing the concept of the person of the Holy Spirit. But it wasn't a foreign idea that came from nowhere. An advocate is a representative, much like a priest, who stands to help resolve issues and conflicts between two parties. In Jesus' explanation, The Advocate would be given to those who believe in him so they could have direct access to interact with his Father. No longer would an outside or third party need to be employed to take up a matter.

Implementing change is one of the most difficult aspects of leadership. Countless books have been written about the subject, especially on leading change within an organization. The older a person gets, the harder it becomes to change. Ideas become engrained. Routines and patterns become firmly established over time. This is understandable since there is safety and comfort attached to doing things a certain way. From my experience of working in the restaurant, breakfast was the most difficult meal of the day to prepare. Guests would have the most unusual requests for how they wanted their food prepared. I remember the guest who asked for two eggs, one scrambled, the other over easy, with extra crispy bacon on a separate plate. Then there are the coffee orders, which are a nightmare in themselves. Try to remember *light roast decaf Americano with frothed oat milk and a little puff of whipped cream.* My theory on why people are so picky at breakfast is that the morning hour is a daily disruption. A person is tired, cranky, and possibly off to a job they don't like. Therefore, the need for a predictable treat to anticipate creates a little semblance of control and certainty. This is part of why change is difficult to encourage and difficult to adopt. The adage, "If it ain't broke, don't fix it" is completely sensible. If extra crispy bacon on a separate plate works for you, why would I ask or expect you to consider another presentation?

To Better Wine

The best approach I have found to encouraging change is understanding the reticence in a person even to consider change. To ask someone to change is to expect them to admit that the way they have been doing things is wrong. And to admit wrong of any kind can feel like an impossible task. But if you move the encouragement to change out of the realm of right or wrong and present it from a place of improvement and betterment, the possibility for success in leading change is increased.

With so much change coming on the horizon, Jesus knew it would be very difficult for some of His followers to grasp a different way of belief. He explained that it was better for them if He went away. They would be better off if he left so that another one could take over and do a much better job than he did. In fact, Jesus was willing and ready to step out of the way because the role of Advocate was not his to exercise. To consider change, I must first see what I stand to gain.

Change involves giving up a way of behaving. And in the case of Jesus' followers, they would be asked to give up a sense of security in a religious system they had known their whole lives. And the keepers of this system weren't very lenient or kind. To seriously consider the words of this Astounding Teacher, this change might even cost them their lives. So how could it be better if he went away?

All change must be seen through the lens of what I stand to gain. This is one of the two requisites for a life of faith, as noted in Hebrews:

> *And without faith it is impossible to please God, because anyone who comes to him must believe that he exists and that he rewards those who earnestly seek him.*
>
> Hebrews 11:6

To have faith in The Almighty is to believe The One exists and that there is reward in the process. Without these two elements, faith does not thrive. Faith needs an author—a starting point, an origin. It always begins with an invitation to believe and trust that The Source is true and that everything spoken by it is worthy of being followed. But The Author of Our Faith doesn't expect us to stop there. We are not expected to blindly follow along simply because we were told we should or because we thought we would end up in hell if we didn't. Instead, The Author invites us into a better life than the one we are living. The Author's kindness includes a sense of reward for our decision to respond to the invitation. Reward is always a result of pursuing the life of faith.

Why would reward be a key part of the life of faith? Why should I expect anything from my choice to follow My Maker wholeheartedly? This can sound a little selfish, like I'm only in it for the money. Shouldn't my devotion be enough? Why should I expect anything in return when I owe everything I am to The One who died for me?

So why stop there? Why stop with receiving the gift of salvation and not take hold of the riches of the inheritance made available to all the people of faith? If my faith only makes room for the metaphor of Savior with the only gift as salvation, then I miss out on the rewards of moving in the metaphor of Gracious Father.

> *I pray that the eyes of your heart may be enlightened in order that you may know the hope to which he has called you, the riches of his glorious inheritance in his holy people,*
>
> Ephesians 1:18

The metaphor of Savior includes more than just salvation, more than just the act of being taken from a place of shame in the past and now brought into right standing with The Almighty. It should always expand into the metaphor of Gracious Father. The Savior made a way for children to return home to the place that was made for us within that home. This new place is filled with all the blessings a father would want to lavish on his beloved children. And for a child to refuse the father is to keep his love at arm's length and stubbornly say, "I don't deserve any of this." No good father wants to hear his children say something like that. No good father wants to keep that kind of distance from his children.

Metaphor isn't intended to be one size fits all. We will need many metaphors along the way if we are to begin to scratch the surface of the nature and intention of The One Who Loves Us Most. And our ability to hold them simultaneously will be to our benefit. In the book of Ecclesiastes, it is said:

It is good to grasp the one, and not let go of the other.

Ecclesiastes 7:18

Wisdom invites us to make room for many thoughts and ideas, even when they might be paradoxical or incongruent. How can God be both my father and my judge? How can I be considered both a servant and a friend of Jesus? How can I expect to live as wise as serpents and innocent as doves? Such is the importance of being able to understand and embrace metaphor. Faith allows me to move in and out of these identities. With the guidance of The Advocate, I need not worry if I am doing it right. The Advocate will be ever present with me, keeping me in line with my new faith and not with an old law.

Today's faith
Cannot be spoken of
In yesterday's language

Faith
Needs words
That haven't
Been spoken yet

In the meantime
Always
Be listening
For the
Vocabulary of heaven

Some of us

Don't fight

The good fight

Because

We identify

As lovers

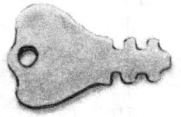

CHAPTER 6

BEYOND THE METAPHOR

Eventually, there comes a point when metaphor isn't enough to comprehend the complexity and majesty of The Glorious One. The imagery in the apocalyptic literature is a case in point—images of dragons and beasts with multiple heads and horns, with additional features that resemble a leopard, a bear, and a lion. These are mysterious images and using them within the limitations of our language is confusing. Here's what I do when I come up against metaphors in the text that I can't decipher.

Four Considerations

Mark Twain famously said:

> *It ain't those parts of the Bible that I can't understand that bother me, it is the parts that I do understand.*

While I attended seminary, Dean Cate was one of the voices who assured me it is okay to live with mystery and uncertainty. While I need not shy away from contemplating these mysteries, at some point, I will discover I don't have access to a vast realm of knowledge when it comes to understanding the nature of my Creator. Is it possible that I can know what was in the mind of God upon the creation of the universe? Can I fathom the great mysteries that are within The Almighty? Is it possible for me to understand his motive? My answer to these questions is yes and no.

The Secret Things

The scripture gives us clues along the way to the nature of Our Creator. I would start with this clue first from the book of Deuteronomy:

> *The secret things belong to the Lord our God, but the things revealed belong to us and to our children forever, that we may follow all the words of this law.*
>
> Deuteronomy 29:29

This is to acknowledge that the finite mind cannot conceive of all the ways of Our Creator. There will be things that can be known about The One Who Reveals, and other aspects of The Mysterious One that will remain a secret mystery. This is why metaphor is indispensable in our comprehension of The Divine. We will only get things partly right. When Jesus says, *"the Kingdom of Heaven is like . . ."* he admits that the word picture will be inadequate and won't capture its entirety, but it will be a good starting point for it to begin to make sense to his listener. And it will be sufficient for faith to take hold of as it grows into maturity of understanding.

The Boundary of Time

Another mystery to grasp and hold in tension is the concept of time in the Kingdom of Heaven. The apostle Peter reminded his listeners about time:

> *But do not forget this one thing, dear friends: With the Lord a day is like a thousand years, and a thousand years are like a day.*
>
> 2 Peter 3:8

The Ancient of Days exists outside of time and dwells in eternity where there are no clocks. The One is eternal, and His Kingdom exists as such. The One has no other reference point. It makes sense that The One is also known as I AM. So much meaning can be sussed out from those three letters. The I AM is now, has always been, and always will be now. There is no past tense to I AM. Nor does I AM have a future. The One Who is Ever Present just simply is.

But we, the creation of I AM, have been set within a world bound by time. We have a beginning, and we all will have an end. Each person is born at a point in time and eventually dies at a future point. That lifespan is measured in units of time. Years, days, hours, and minutes. My dad was born on

September 15, 1930, and passed away on August 20, 2005. We say he was seventy-five years old when he died.

But the Ancient of Days has no birthday and will never pass away.

The sense of what we know as time is another boundary constructed for the sake of creation. Time is a created element just like the air we breathe and the water we drink, wash in, and float upon. We were given fire to warm ourselves and light our path. And earth was created to ground us and support our feet. In order to make sense of The Ancient of Days, the metaphor cannot be fathomed without embracing both the mysterious nature of I AM and the fact that I AM is not confined to time.

The Place Outside of Time

A third mysterious consideration to ponder is to ask when the prophetic activity written about in the scripture regarding the heavenly realm actually happened. We can only think in chronological terms because time is our inescapable boundary. But when John the Revelator wrote this description, it forces one to stop and think:

> *All inhabitants of the earth will worship the beast—all whose names have not been written in the Lamb's book of life, the Lamb who was slain from the creation of the world.*
>
> Revelation 13:8

How could this be possible? How could Jesus have been slain before the beginning of creation? I can't pretend to give a full defense of this statement but must factor in the equation that the Kingdom of Heaven isn't bound by time, but my world is. So where does that leave me? It leaves me with a mystery I can't possibly solve because there is data I can't access. I don't live outside of time. Time is all I know. And if I refuse to admit there is a world I know nothing about, my faith will never make room for the impossible because I'm only concerned about what I can see. And faith is all about the unseen.

The War in Heaven

A fourth consideration I must hold as I put my faith in I AM is the presence of a conflict in the heavenly realm that I can't see. The text refers to it as the war in heaven (Rev. 12:7). There was an angel who rebelled against the Holy One and set a conflict in motion. Isaiah's metaphor for this rebellious angel is The Morning Star (Isa. 14:12). Ezekiel's language refers to The Guardian Cherub (Eze. 29:16). Jesus said, "I saw Satan fall like lightning from heaven. (Luke 10:18). Here he uses another metaphor to help us picture the mystery. Peter called the fallen angel a Roaring Lion seeking to devour. Peculiar that this Roaring Lion was cast down to earth (Isa. 14:12).

So why on earth? Why cast down the Fallen One here? It seems to be inviting more problems. But we must ask this question right along with our previous question: Why did The Creator impose a law with the inevitability that the law would be broken?

As a human, it's second nature for me to answer these from a human perspective bound by time. I can write it off as insane and dismiss The Creator as a strange autocrat who seems to want to stir up trouble. But this is too easy a conclusion for me to make.

New Wineskins

I freely admit my lack of understanding of many things when it comes to spiritual matters. My journey has been a process of rediscovering and recovering the tender places in my heart that have been there since I was a child. I was a very sensitive and creative kid growing up, and that nature never escaped me. In adulthood, it took years before I could accept that the way I viewed the world was actually a gift and not a liability. I often offer young, newly minted dads this bit of advice:

> *Whatever you see in your little child right now is who they are. They aren't old enough to know how to ignore their nature. But eventually the world will try to beat it out of them, and your job as dad is to watch over that tender-hearted child. And if they wander from it, you will know the place to help them return to.*

A late-in-life idea that helped me understand this role is the word *attunement*. Think of this word like dialing in a station on a radio. To hear what is being broadcast, I need to be attuned to a particular frequency. If not, I'm going to miss the ballgame or the music I am seeking to enjoy. My father was attuned to me. He recognized my creative energy and didn't stand in the way of it. He loved to tell the story of me trying to imitate one of my heroes, Evel Knievel. He was a daredevil of my time who jumped over cars, trucks, and buses on a Harley-Davidson motorcycle. Dad often regaled the time he came around the corner of the garage to see me flying by him six feet in the air as I launched my single-speed Schwinn bicycle over a makeshift plywood ramp. I don't know if I was really six feet in the air, but I loved how he loved telling the story about me. He didn't try to squelch that youthful drive out of fear that I would hurt myself. Instead, he encouraged that energy and gave me space to experiment and flourish.

The Gift of Poetry

But this wasn't always the case. As I began my life of faith, there was very little room for creative expression in the faith communities of which I was a part. There was a strong emphasis on rational arguments. Academic and intellectual defense of the faith was of high value and logic and reason were elevated above music and creativity. I would never say these things are un-important. They were not the core principles within which my faith would thrive. It would take many more years for me to see the difference and make a conscious effort to pursue one over the other. I would not dismiss or deny the more left-brain approach. I would return to the creative energy that was still inside me.

It wasn't until I was fifty-six years old that I uncovered the power of poetry and learned how to access it as a means of self-expression and self-dis-covery. I had gone a lifetime without knowing the beauty available. But to be fair, I wasn't in a place to find it until I was fifty-six, widowed, unemployed, and displaced from much of what I found secure. It took these circumstances to focus the eyes of my heart to see what I couldn't see at any other time in my life. Viewing it this way shields me from feeling ashamed and living in a "what if" mentality. What if I had paid attention to poetry when I was younger? I can't live in that kind of retrospective review. I can't change the past. But I can anticipate the future. And poetry is shaping my future self.

In March of my fifty-sixth year, I took a solo trip to Ireland. A friend had recommended a book of poetry by Irish poet John O'Donohue. I bought a copy for the trip and decided I wouldn't open it until I was in country. I boarded a train from Dublin to Galway, surrounded by all the romance of Ireland. The creaking sound of the passenger train pulling away from Heuston station, along with the view of Irish architecture from my forefacing window seat seemed like a good time to pull out that book and read. I pulled down the tray table and opened the book.

I couldn't get past the first five poems.

The beauty was too much to contain. O'Donohue had assembled words in a way I had never encountered. It was as if his reflections on love and loss, grief and sorrow were a direct message to me, a grieving man wandering through the beauty of this author's home country. I wept tears I didn't know were possible. And I felt emotions that I didn't know existed. Even now, I struggle for words to explain the experience. I can only trust that the spirit of what I am trying to convey here is received in a commensurate way.

I stayed with those five poems for the remainder of the trip. I didn't read anything else in the book. Those poems meant so much to me; I didn't want to leave them until I had extracted everything I could. When I returned home, I took out my old Remington Quiet-Riter manual typewriter. I typed a quote from the book, took a picture of it, and posted it on my Instagram account. After about thirty minutes, I felt a pang of regret in my spirit. Not for plagiarism, because I credited John O'Donohue, but because The Still Small Voice said, "That's too easy. You should write your own."

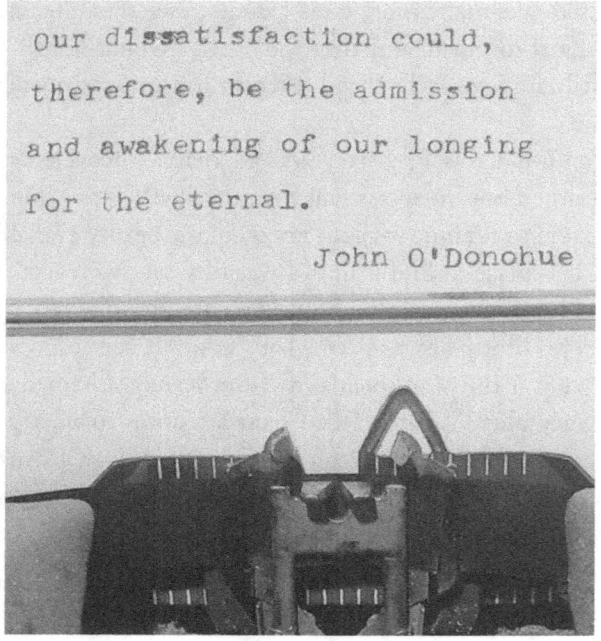

The next day, I took out a blank sheet of paper, rolled it into the carriage, and typed these three lines:

Half a mile from nowhere

Took all day to get here

Got half a mind to turn around

It was the opening lyrics to a song I had written for a wedding twenty years prior. It was my original work, and I was a bit sheepish about posting it. But the journey of a thousand miles starts with the first step, and I could tell this was a new direction for my writing. I had never written poetry before, but I approached it like all my other writing. I would write to myself first. I would write out of my own experiences and not try to imitate another writer. I would attempt to write and post daily but would not let myself feel compelled if there was nothing to say.

Over time, my Instagram followers started to notice the change in my writing, and the feedback was endearing, not because it felt good to have an audience but because my words were landing differently. I was speaking a new language—the language of poetry—and I could see that I was expressing something within me that needed to continue. It was no longer just a writing exercise. I could now see it as a gift to be shared and opened. So, I continued to write and post. I tried not to overthink it. Even if I wasn't fully convinced it was worth posting, I would post anyway. I decided I would not decide for my readers if it was worthy. I would let them decide for themselves. Through this process, I started to see the reason I needed to keep writing. As I sought to see if I could synthesize difficult ideas into a few lines of words, the results started to become clear. Readers began letting me know what my words meant to them. Because of this feedback, I started to hone my focus and take my typewriting more seriously.

About a year into this writing project, my editor asked me if I was saving all those bits of thought. I told her they were all still in a stack in the order that I'd typed them, and I hadn't done anything with them. She asked if she could see them. I went home and gathered the typed papers in a stack. There were 575 pages. I put them in a box and made the handoff. She asked to sit with them for a bit and get back to me after she read them.

A couple of weeks later, we met for coffee, and she brought the pages, except they were now organized—thirteen separate stacks, paperclipped together, each with a yellow sticky note with one word. The top one was Grief, followed by Loss, Sadness, Joy, Anger, and so on. As she handed them back, she said, "This is what you've been doing. You've been processing the death of your wife, and this is how it comes out of you. You have a gift of communicating concise thoughts and I think you have a book in here." And thus, from the thirteen bundles came my second book, a book of poetry and thought.

I relay this story to describe the process of validating my way of handling mystery. I was not encouraged to write through my grief. I did what came naturally. And once I had established a rhythm to it, that pattern was recognized for what it was doing. It took me fifty-six years to discover a particular gift of communicating. Had it always been lying there latent, or was it a brand-new development forged through the experience of personal pain and loss?

It was not easy for me to use the word "gift" when referring to my writing. It felt arrogant to say aloud that I have a gift. I would rather let someone else tell me that. I don't feel confident telling it to myself. Much of the reticence came from my early years of faith development. When I was in college, I taught myself how to play guitar. But spiritual mentors never encouraged that pursuit, telling me it was a distraction, and it might take me away from taking my faith seriously. The same was said of playing golf and other activities deemed frivolous or a waste of time. Deep in my brain, a seed was sown that grew into a tangled vine of contempt that choked out my creative drive. Or at least it made me second-guess it. Even many years later, at fifty-six, I still felt a bit of guilt to admit that I had a gift for communicating.

With the help of consistent counseling, I started getting in touch with the repressed creativity I carried inside. I started asking myself this important personal question:

Who benefits from me denying that I have a gift?

I would journal regularly from this starting question. I asked myself over and over: what is the value of downplaying the gift I want to offer? Where is the benefit of not taking what I have been given and making it available? My journaling eventually revealed the payoff: If I stayed quiet, I would not have to face the possibility of criticism or put-downs by a disapproving voice. As I reflected more, I could see that these are common struggles. I am no different than anyone else. It seems like everyone has a level of creative insecurity in some form. Maybe sharing my gift might encourage someone else to do the same with theirs. It may not be writing, but you know exactly what your gift is. And in reading this, there may be a stirring inside you that bears witness to what I am saying.

The Kingdom of Heaven is constantly in the process of producing new wine and looks to pour it out on the earth below. This metaphor is an incredibly helpful lens through which to view our giftedness. The new wine is the new way of understanding this Kingdom that is always improving. Unlike an earthly vineyard, where there are good years and bad ones, The Kingdom continues to pour out new and better wine with each vintage. And The Vine Keeper is always looking for a fresh stock of wineskins to pour it into.

Your gift may be one of those new wineskins. The old ones from which you once drank were fine for the previous season. To acknowledge the need for new wineskins has nothing to do with devaluing the place of the previous. Jesus himself said:

> *And no one pours new wine into old wineskins. Otherwise, the new wine will burst the skins; the wine will run out and the wineskins will be ruined.*
>
> Luke 5:37

To not look for new wineskins is to minimize the merit and worth of the coming vintage. What the Kingdom wants to pour out will be ruined without citizens who see, by faith, the need for fresh, new wineskins to preserve it. If any of this stirs you, don't dismiss it. And don't just take my word for it. Ask The Advocate for insight. He was sent for this very reason. Time is irrelevant in the Kingdom of Heaven. It is not wise to look back and wish or wonder. We only have the present as we look ahead to the future and dream about what can be.

The Artist and The Craftsman

The need for new wineskins is why I believe the time of The Artist is nigh. And here is how I distinguish between art and craft. Bear with me, as this is an oversimplification of two immense and beautiful activities. Both art and craft are interested in creating, but each has a different motivation. At its core, art is interested in creating something new, whereas craft is bent on creating something in the same fashion as before. The skilled craftsman is much like a baker in the kitchen. At the end of the shift, she wants to bake 100 loaves of bread that look perfectly identical. This replication process invokes a discipline of paying attention to details, techniques, and methods meant to yield the same result. The table built by a craftsman will look different from the table constructed by an artist. Likely, no two tables of the artist will ever be alike, with every project being original. There are metaphors in scripture that take note of both. This example is from Zechariah 1:20:

> *Then the Lord showed me four craftsmen. I asked, "What are these coming to do?" He answered, "These are the horns that scattered Judah so that no one could raise their head, but the craftsmen have come to terrify them and throw down these horns of the nations who lifted up their horns against the land of Judah to scatter its people."*

What is the meaning of the four craftsmen here? Why was this metaphor used to describe an effort to terrify the Lord's enemies? What does a craftsman have to do with being a soldier? My take is this. Is there any more patient person than a craftsman? His painstaking attention to detail requires an extra portion of forbearance and self-restraint. And since patience is a fruit of The Advocate, the Prince of this World has none. Think of the patient people you know. Do they sometimes seem so at ease that they don't appear to care about the things that have you hot and bothered? Even the smallest bit of patience can irk the pushy, impulsive person who doesn't want to wait on anything having to do with process. This is how the craftsman can defeat the opposition just by being patient. Therefore, within the metaphor of a craftsman, I can discern something of what The Prophet, Priest, and King had in mind through this prophecy.

And while the craftsman plays a significant role in the realm of faith, the artist does also, but in a different way. The Spirit of Prophecy spoke to Isaiah of their desire to do something new.

See, the former things have taken place, and new things I declare; before they spring into being I announce them to you."

Isaiah 42:9

I've always taken literally that The Originator of Art wants to do something new, something that has never been seen or done before. This impulse is set within the heart of the artist, who was made in The Creator's image. When the artist reads Isaiah 42:9, he will read it differently than a craftsman. The artist immediately begins to envision possibilities and new works. Within this territory, the faith of the artist can thrive. Faith trades in the currency of the unknown. Faith is being sure and certain of what cannot be seen, and thus, the artist's heart begins to beat faster, and his blood begins to pump. It knows it was born for this.

I believe the artist has an important role within the twenty-first-century expression of The Church of the Future. Within The Church as I Once Knew It, there wasn't a high value for artistic communication. There were other gifts at the time that were more relevant to the mindset of a modern, technological world. The metaphors that made sense in the '50s, '60s, and '70s are not able to encompass the thinking of a postmodern social structure. We were putting people into space and on the moon and making huge scientific discoveries that would change the way every human lived.

In seminary, we studied the past great revivals and awakenings. And every class and lecture seemed to focus on the same thing: *What are the earmarks of revival?* The professor wanted us to be acquainted with the commonalities of past movements as we looked and prayed toward a similar outpouring in our current days. On February 8, 2023, a spontaneous surge of prayer and worship broke out among a gathering of students at Asbury University in Wilmore, Kentucky. It continued around the clock for two more weeks until it wound to a close on February 24, 2023. It was heralded as a revival that was sure to sweep the nation. People from all over the world traveled to the little Kentucky town, curious to see for themselves this story that was making the news on all the cable outlets. It seemed to attract anyone with an iPhone and a microphone, and makeshift podcasts were assembled and uploaded to share their take on this thing that was causing such an uproar. As you would imagine, there were detractors and critics, worried this was nothing more than an emotional outpouring that didn't have the true earmarks of revival. But the signs people were looking for and the manifestations of what we were taught to observe didn't include the description in Isaiah:

See, the former things have taken place, and new things I declare.

                                                                Isaiah 42:9

The outpouring at Asbury wasn't new. Wikipedia records at least eight out-
pourings beginning in 1905 and repeating in 1908, 1921, 1950, 1958, 1970,
1992, and 2006 before the 2023 expression. It may appear that I am dismissing the past goings on. That isn't the case. I'm all for anything that moves the
needle from cold to hot in the realm of faith. But my fascination is with the
new things spoken of in Isaiah. What is the new thing? This is what I have
committed myself to watching for.

The prophet uses additional metaphor to describe the new thing.

*See, I am doing a new thing! Now it springs up; do you not perceive it? I
am making a way in the wilderness and streams in the wasteland.*

                                                                Isaiah 43:19

Isaiah was shown that the new thing he wrote about would be akin to someone putting a road in the wilderness and a source of flowing water in the
desert. I take this to mean that The Creator of All Things New wants to put
useful things in places where they otherwise don't belong. Imagine being lost
and wandering out in the middle of nowhere and coming up on a four-lane
interstate cutting through an impossible pass. Picture being stranded in the
desert, and just over the next dune, you see a beautiful river of clean water that
flows as far as the eye can see. It would be something completely unexpected
but readily welcomed by the weary, sun-scorched drifter who may have given
up hope. Again, I speak no ill against awakenings, revivals, and movements
in any form. They are realms within which the faith of many will thrive; but
for me, I yearn for something new.

The Jesus Movement in the United States was a unique spiritual response
to the culture during a time of disillusionment over war. But I didn't grow
up seeing that blunt, in-your-face, confrontational approach to evangelism as
effective as some did. Yet I was taught how to use that method nearly twenty
years past its sell-by date. My leaders assured me this is how people came to
faith back in the day and doubled down on the efficacy of the methodology. I
was taught how to go out on the streets on a Friday or Saturday night and talk
to people outside of bars about their faith. In the years I tried that, not one
single person made a decision. In fact, very few were even interested. But the
adopted metaphor of saving souls from an eternity in hell was very effective

in inducing enough guilt in my conscience to keep going back out into the night weekend after weekend.

I'm a country boy at heart. I grew up on a twenty-six-acre farm in rural northwest Oklahoma. I hated it as a kid because I was so lonely with no neighbor kids around to play with. But by osmosis, I absorbed the beauty of the outdoors and developed a fascination with nature. This is why I could never thrive in a major urban environment. I love visiting a big city, but I would never want to live there. I could exist there, but I would not thrive. I need access to wide-open spaces. I want to see the sky without buildings around the perimeter of my vision. I need a little dirt to dig and put seeds in and watch grow into flowers and vegetables that end up on my table. But my friends living in high-rise towers and moving within the skyscraper corridors of Manhattan or Chicago wouldn't live anywhere else. This is what I mean by watching and waiting for something new that The Breath of The Spirit moves along. I hope many more Asbury's happen because they will be helpful and foundational for someone like me who caught the Wind of Faith at an early age. Over these years, I have grown to understand where my faith wants to live, and I will pitch my tent there.

Solomon spoke this word of wisdom that has been helpful to me:

> Do not say, "Why were the old days better than these?" For it is not wise to ask such questions.
>
> Ecclesiastes 7:10

We often refer to the *"good old days"* as a way of remembering a time in our past. Typically, it is spoken of in a spirit of nostalgia coupled with a wish to return to a previous and preferred way of life. Solomon labeled this pining unwise. Looking backward with fondness is different from yearning to return to it. Good memories tie us to the endearing influences on our story, but they can also keep us distant from a flourishing faith by wanting to go back.

In my hometown there is a teaching ministry called Back to The Bible. At one time, it broadcasted sermons and messages all over the world. I remember my grandmother listening to their programs on her AM radio when I was a kid. The metaphor was centered around the idea that society has wandered away from the Bible and would do well to return to a time when the Bible was revered and respected, its teaching read and obeyed. You might be asking, "Where is the problem here? Wouldn't anyone benefit from getting back into reading the Bible?" I would answer there is nothing wrong with the action, but the metaphor might need an upgrade.

We all have habits that are good to maintain. Take exercise as an example. I would guess most people, even those who are very physically fit, have had seasons of ebb and flow when it comes to the consistency of their workouts. You may have run marathons when you were in your twenties, and now, in your forties, you feel the toll of age and time on your body. You can't go back twenty years. You can't run at forty-five like you could at twenty-five. But instead of accepting the change, you decide to double down and try to get back to that time when you could run eighty miles a week. One reason this isn't wise is those days can never be repeated. You were unique in that season of your life, and now, it is time to move forward as a runner, not backward. You love running and hope to enjoy it for a long, long time. Therefore, you must look ahead to what changes are needed right now to ensure you are still running at fifty-five, sixty-five, and seventy-five. Trying to reproduce the results you achieved at twenty-five will eventually lead to breakdown and injury. So instead of taking on a metaphor that tells you to Just Go Back and Do It, a better mental picture would be to Look Forward and Run to The Future. I believe this is why Solomon opined that it isn't wise to try to go back and wish for bygone days.

It's very important to understand how the metaphors we adopt shape our view of the world. And they are very telling. Some personalities like the metaphor of the grind. They love to equate every day with continually grinding out something productive. Get up early and grind at the gym, grind away at work, and grind away at the next career opportunity. *Rise and Grind* is posted on their Instagram feed as motivation to keep them going. Hustle is another metaphorical word that fits here. People speak of having a side hustle or keeping up the hustle in order to get and stay ahead. This metaphor works for some, creating a boundary within which their faith can thrive. I am not one who identifies with this image, but neither am I saying it's wrong. My faith needs a different pasture through which it can roam and graze.

A metaphor is a snapshot, a picture worth a thousand words. I would add that it is a partial glimpse, never intended to be the only image our imagination gets wrapped around. A communicator might use several metaphors to convey a point so the audience can have a clearer view of the message. Let's revisit how Jesus did this when he said, "The Kingdom of Heaven is like . . . ." Here are three times he made the comparison with the use of a metaphor, which is commonly known as a parable.

The Kingdom of Heaven is like a mustard seed, which a man took and planted in his field.

Matthew 13:31

The Kingdom of Heaven is like yeast that a woman took and mixed into about sixty pounds of flour until it worked all through the dough.

Matthew 13:33

"The Kingdom of Heaven is like treasure hidden in a field.

Matthew 13:44

A mustard seed, some yeast, and a treasure hidden in a field. How are these three separate items with unique characteristics useful to build a bridge of understanding? I would submit that Jesus likes to engage the imagination of the listener and that imagination is necessary for faith. Every person listening to his words would have been familiar with mustard seeds, yeast, and the wish to find hidden treasure. They could visualize the tiniest of seeds growing into a tree. I would guess every person hearing his words knew how bread was made and how yeast transformed the dough. And who wouldn't want to find a hidden treasure, and have it change their life?

The book of Ephesians intimates this:

Now to him who is able to do immeasurably more than all we ask or imagine, according to his power that is at work within us, to him be glory in the church and in Christ Jesus throughout all generations, for ever and ever! Amen.

Ephesians 3:20

If the Author of our Faith can do more than we ask or imagine, the implication here is that we are already engaged in asking and imagining. The Giver of Dreams won't go past our wildest dreams unless we start with them. Dreams exist in the realm of imagination, and metaphor is the language of that principality. In my early faith development, I was never encouraged to imagine, and now I wouldn't know what to do without it. Imagination shouldn't be limited to childhood. To imagine and dream is indispensable in creating the better future. The artist is integral in the process of seeing the new things materialize from the Kingdom of Heaven. And the art of metaphor is needed to imagine how the new art is to be revealed.

Take, for example, the use of sports metaphor to get a point across. I've heard this one used often by pastors who feel their congregations are not enthusiastic enough. The rebuke might start with comparing how excited you get when your favorite sports team wins its championship game, but you barely will sing in church, let alone clap your hands. Like the grind, this may make sense and work for some, but it's not a good metaphorical comparison for me. In my imagination, the life of faith isn't even remotely like watching a sporting event, but this is only my point of view. I am writing from my own experience, through the guidance of The Advocate, about considering metaphors that allow my faith to thrive.

When I first saw the art of Blue Man Group in Las Vegas in 2000, I had no idea what I had just witnessed. It was art of the truest form. It was brand new, unlike anything I had ever consumed. After the show was over, I knew I had seen something important, but I had no words for the profundity of this moment and how it would begin to shape my future career direction. I stayed in my seat, reveling in the spectacle, until the usher asked me to leave so they could begin cleaning the theater. I walked out alone onto the Vegas strip, my head seeming to spin from the assault of cacophonic sound and pummeling of visual imagery. It would take several days before I could synthesize the art of Blue Man Group and reckon it as a modern-day parable for me.

If you have never seen their stage production, there is no good way to explain what it is or what it's about. One entertainment writer dubbed it "The Omnisexual Promise Keepers for The New Millennium." And what does that mean?!? It makes about as much sense as any description would, but it falls short of hitting the mark. Just go ahead and apply some whatever and call it good.

After several days, this was my summation: A Blue Man Group show is both a celebration and mockery of pop culture. It invites the audience to laugh at itself while simultaneously offering a subliminal invitation to think about something greater than confetti and massive rolls of toilet paper strewn about the seats and aisles. Their deep summons to me was in the form of this question:

> *Who is going to live your life? Are you going to live it, or will you let someone else live it for you?*

I was at a crossroads in my faith when I encountered this art, and just like my foray into Irish poetry, I knew I needed to let it shape and change me. My conclusion: I can't go to sleep on what I believe. I knew I would have a choice to make about my role as a paid member of my vocational ministry career. I knew it would have to come to an end if I was going to live my own life and not let the history and traditions of my past decide for me.

I don't write this book as a new mandate. I write it to set someone free. The current metaphors that have built The Church as We Know It are fine for many. And if your faith thrives there, there is no need to change. But if your faith seems flaccid and unaroused, it might be time for a different metaphor.

Your faith
Has grown
So far beyond
From where it started
That some
Who knew you
At the beginning
Think you have
Wandered from it

But

Love the good love

Doesn't have

The same ring to it

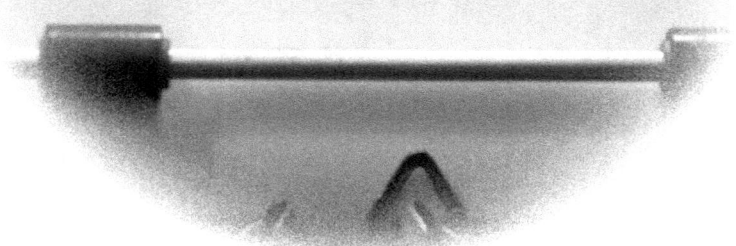

CHAPTER 7

FAITH THAT DOESN'T NEED DEFENDING

Love the Good Love

Some of us don't need a new faith. We are convinced there is someone greater than ourselves. We feel it in our bones. We've sensed the nearness of The Advocate. We see the night sky. We feel the heat of the sun. We are in awe of the detail of a fragrant rose situated among a stem of thorns. We feel the crush of the ocean waves and revel in our smallness as we stand on top of a mountain. These details in every place we look seem to be the very fingerprints of an Everlasting Creator we long to know. Our frustration stems from the small, limited language we were given that never seemed to be a dialect that could adequately communicate the beauty that has captured our hearts.

No, we didn't need a new faith. We just needed a different metaphor.

Take the language surrounding faith of the spiritual community in which I was reared. My mentors cajoled my belief that I must always be ready to make a defense of the things I believe. They went on to help me believe that my faith would be subject to attack by the spirit of the age. As a teenager new to his faith, it never occurred to me that I should examine this line of thinking. If my faith constantly needs to be defended, shouldn't I be concerned? What does this say about faith? Is it that fragile? Must I live in fear that I am one step away from throwing in the towel because I didn't defend it properly?

I defend what is weak and vulnerable. And those are not words I associate with the strength of faith. If this is the underlying quality of faith, why did I sign up for a belief I had to prop up constantly? It didn't make sense. That's why I needed a different metaphor for my faith.

Defense in the form of fighting is the right metaphor for some, but others of us don't fight the good fight. I remember the friends in high school who always seemed to be itching for a fight. One guy would constantly pick on me just to get a response. Never mind that he hated being ignored, and I couldn't ignore him forever. His bullying would eventually push me to the edge, and I would try to fight back. He was bigger, stronger, and angrier than me and always ended up on top of me, shoving my face in the dirt. I was defenseless, and fighting was not the way I was going to solve this problem.

Consider this. If I am always fighting with my world, will it ever trust me when I offer it a drink of water or bandage its wounded heart? If the neighbor with whom I am constantly engaged in a fight is ever in dire need, have I already lost my opportunity to help because of my need to fight back? The way I face my world is the way my world will face me. If I face my world in a combative stance, my world will face me ready to fight. If I face my world with an eye of judgment, my world will be eager to point and say I told you so when I fail. If I face my world like it is out to get me, it will most certainly be out to get me.

But if I face my world with an air of kindness, my world will be forced to address my kindness.

If I believe my world has power over me, then I will face my world from a position of defensiveness, with my fists up and not my hands out to help. The metaphor of fighting the good fight might still be useful, but I'll picture something different than defending with fists, guns, and warfare. If I live from a place of constant security, not constant war, will I be less defensive?

There is a metaphor of warfare spoken of in the text, but I think its nature gets misappropriated.

> *For our struggle is not against flesh and blood, but against the rulers, against the authorities, against the powers of this dark world and against the spiritual forces of evil in the heavenly realms.*
>
> Ephesians 6:12

This warfare isn't a reference to a fight between God and Satan. This is a ridiculous thought. That is not even a fair fight. The Morning Star has fallen, has been defeated, and no longer holds authority. Jesus claimed that right on the cross and announced it to his followers as he was ready to depart and hand over the reins to The Advocate. He said:

All authority in heaven and on earth has been given to me.

Matthew 28:18

To win at war is to destroy and annihilate the enemy. Winning may come through surrender, but a ceasefire doesn't change the heart of the enemy. The spiritual warfare that ensues is no longer about winning. Victory has already been decided. It is now about reigning and exercising the new authority. And The Advocate is delighted now to show us more than Jesus was ever able to reveal during his thirty-three years on earth.

———————————

Prayer
Is an invitation
Not an obligation
And the only way
To do it wrong
Is to give up

If I engage
In prayer
Looking only
For the answers
It's the same
As me planting
An apple tree
And expecting
To pick apples
Tomorrow

If I am

Always fighting

With my world

Will it ever

Trust me

When I offer it

A drink of water

Or bandage

Its wounded heart?

CHAPTER 8

PRAYER THAT DOESN'T WORK

I don't write that title to create controversial attention or to be sensational. I despise clickbait on the internet, and I don't care to participate in furthering that deceptive craft. Instead, I want to point out how The Most Gracious One took the lid off a restrictive metaphor through which I viewed the practice of prayer.

I intentionally mention and admit my bias in this book because I accept that I often operate with an incomplete picture or upon a fraction of the truth. But as I've grown in my faith, I've gained new insight and understanding through the wisdom of The Ancient of Days that expands my perspective, allowing my faith more room to stretch out and thrive. Acknowledging personal bias fosters humility and curiosity. To admit I don't know everything about everything is a good place to be. It's a place of security and peace. It says I'm not in charge and can rest in The One Who Is.

Life is full of great mysteries. And some of those mysteries will be solved eventually, like when it was assumed that the earth is flat. But others will still leave us confounded, regardless of time, effort, and resources thrown at them. Consider this poem in the book of Proverbs:

> *There are three things*
> *that are too amazing for me*
> *four that I do not understand:*
>
> *the way of an eagle in the sky*
> *the way of a snake on a rock*

the way of a ship on the high seas
and the way of a man with a young woman.

Proverbs 30:19

One can take this list and break it down with the current knowledge base of information that exists in the twenty-first century. You can explain through the law of aerodynamics why an eagle can fly, thanks to our modern understanding of physics. But at the time, it might as well have been magic that made that bird stay up in the air. The snake that wriggles its way across a flat surface also has zoological explanations, and the buoyancy of a large ship has a scientific solution that allows even bigger and bigger boats to sail those high seas today.

But I would argue that the latter element of this poem is the one that will remain a mystery. The beautiful differences between a man and a woman have been studied forever, and still, we are left to wonder why the attraction is so strong. John Gray summed up the difference in the title of his 1992 book, *Men Are from Mars, Women Are from Venus*. The poet and the songwriter probably have the advantage here over the scientist in putting these feelings into discernable words.

I believe Our Creator has granted us permission to search out these mysteries to the degree our heart drives us toward finding an answer. It is in the human DNA to study, to explore, test, design, and imagine our world and surrounding universe. Technology seeks to solve complex problems to improve the quality of life. But there comes a point where I must admit and say out loud, "I just don't know."

The invitation to seek out the mysteries of life is always before us. Jesus used the metaphor of standing in front of a door, saying we always have permission to knock and keep knocking as we wait for it to be opened. I believe this applies to any aspect of human curiosity, whether it is an interest in understanding The Almighty or making a breakthrough in science or medicine. A cure for cancer has not yet been found, but that doesn't stop scientists from their quest to understand and solve this disease that is so prevalent across the planet. Ask and keep on asking. Seek and keep on seeking. Persistent inquisitiveness will lead to alleviating homelessness and renewing drug-wrecked cities. We must hope and keep on hoping.

In Chapter 5 I reflected on a story that Jesus told about prayer, and how to pray and not give up. It is important to understand the bias I once kept when I considered this story. I think it's best described by this difficult incident in my family.

A Sad Story

My niece was preparing for her husband to have heart surgery. The whole family knew it would be a risky procedure, but it had to be attempted or continue to run the risk of more dire consequences later. To cover all the bases, a support thread was set up via smartphones to dispense updates and to solicit prayer for specific needs along the way. Later that evening, I got an urgent message asking for prayer when the situation suddenly turned. "He is coding. Please pray now."

We all prayed for recovery. And the opposite happened.

The next message was not what any of us wanted to hear. Instead of good news, all of us on the family text chain got the dreaded word. He had passed. As I sat in the pain of shock, I could not help but ask why. Why was this our answer? Did we not ask enough? Did we not have enough people on our group chat? What about the persistent widow in the story? Were we not persistent enough? My niece is now a widow. What gives?

I've dealt with my share of loss of life over the years. I knew if I was going to take faith seriously, I would have to grapple with some very hard questions about loss, and this was the next one in the queue. For the sake of my niece and myself, I started to do some uncomfortable contemplation. I had to face the elephant in my room. Does prayer have any relevance? Does anyone out there even hear our pleas for help?

To ask bluntly, does prayer work?

To which I would now answer, no, it doesn't work. I could see my bias through Jesus' story of the judge and widow. I was considering prayer as a mechanism, like operating a machine. I now see it as nurturing a living organism like a plant.

I don't believe prayer works, much like the old clock in my hallway doesn't work. I can wind it with the key, but I can't expect it to start ticking. Neither can I anticipate the predictable chime on the quarter, half, and top of the hour. The clock is broken. It doesn't work.

In the same way, prayer doesn't work. But I still believe in it.

Machines vs Organisms

I've lived in the same house for thirty-two years. When I took ownership in April 1992, there was a little cultivated plot sectioned off in the northeast corner of the backyard. I didn't have to do much to plant a garden that first year. And every year since I've tended that little area with an array of vegetables and flowers to levels of varying success. Never once has any friend, visitor, or guest asked me how my garden works. That's because people have a general understanding of plants.

Plants grow. They don't work.

That's why no one asks me how my garden works. Instead, they want to know *how* I do it. How do I keep the pests away? How do I keep the weeds back? How do I get such colorful produce? How do I know when to plant? Do I do the same thing every year?

These are questions for a gardener, not a mechanic.

Organic life grows. Mechanical devices work.

Herein is the fundamental shift I had to make to understand the ancient practice of a prayer of faith. It doesn't work. It can't work because it is organic, not mechanical. My understanding of My Maker is living and biological, not automated and mechanistic. It is mysterious, not logical. There is no owner's manual with step-by-step instructions and a separate parts list in case something breaks. Some would argue that the scriptures are that guide, but from my vantage point, I would disagree. The sixty-six books of text tell a story that moves and breathes. It doesn't follow orders. If we want to have a dialogue about prayer, I won't have much to say about how it works. But I can tell you how I've seen it grow.

A gardener doesn't have to know botany or own a book on gardening to begin the activity. All that is required is to put seeds in the ground, stand back, and pay attention. As movement begins to be evident, the gardener watches sprouts come up and looks for leaves to expand and roots to sink deeper. As fruit appears, a hand reaches to pluck one and sample it. Joy ensues. A garden has grown. And it helps to have the Great Gardener to show me a thing or two and guide me in the growth process along the way.

And in the thirty-two years I've nurtured a garden, I'm a much better gardener now. I still plant every spring despite last year's hailstorm and tomato blight. I keep trying and keep improving the process. I won't have fruit if I don't plant, just as I won't have answers if I don't pray.

Yes, I believe in prayer. I just don't believe it functions in the way I once assumed it did. The widow appealed to the heartless judge as a human with feelings, even though he didn't show them. She saw him not as a slot machine with eventual odds but as the only possible source to find her answer. She believed in the humanity of the judge by believing if she kept appealing her case, he might eventually relent. She showed faith in her strategy of persistence, not in thinking the machine would eventually payout the jackpot if she played it long enough.

Seeing prayer through this metaphor of a living, growing organism rather than as a predictable mechanism has helped my faith thrive when I don't see the things happen for which I have been asking.

I wrote this poem to help me sort out my thoughts and encourage my niece as she began the grief journey on the trail of her loss.

Here's why
I don't think
Prayer works

I bought an oven
Took it out of the box
Hooked up the gas line
Plugged it in
Followed the instructions
And it worked

Not a helpful way
For me
To imagine prayer

Rather
I like to picture it
Like planting
A tree

I dig a hole
Set it in place
Water it
And watch
And wait

20 years later
It has grown
The birds

Sing in its branches
And I rest
In its shade

Ovens work
Trees grow

Otherwise
My impatience
Is rewarded
My disbelief
Reinforced
When I expect prayer
To work

Come grow
With me
The best
Is yet to come

CHAPTER 9

THE WRETCH WHO'S
PRONE TO WANDER

In churches, at funerals and gatherings all across my country, these words will be sung every day.

> *Amazing grace! how sweet the sound,*
> *That saved a wretch like me![1]*

"Amazing Grace" is a beloved hymn written by John Newton, an Anglican cleric who fought for the abolition of slavery throughout his life in the 1700s. It is a grand song with deep tradition sung with vigor and gusto by countless people regardless of their faith tradition. I bet I could sing all four verses by heart if called upon at a karaoke party.

At the risk of sounding like Grumpy Old Man, I want to address one very alarming word in the opening lyric. It's the word wretch. I've sung it for years, but why have I recently grown increasingly uncomfortable with it?

It's the language of trauma. And in working through my past traumatic events, I have come to understand how they impair my view of myself and my world. Abuse can lead its victim to adopt a very low view of their worth and value. The abuser is often bigger, stronger, and meaner, leaving the victim to resort to a fight or flight response. If fighting back against a more formidable opponent doesn't look like a good option, the victim will succumb to the abuse by agreeing with the abuser. When the victim is called a whore

---

[1] *Newton, John. "Amazing Grace," published 1779.*

or worthless waste of space, eventually, an agreement will be made, and the victim will act in line with these accusations. If the abuser says I'm a piece of shit, what else am I to do other than believe it?

A Wretch like Me

The word "wretch" is a starting point, but it should never be adopted as an identity. The alcoholic knows the trouble his addiction has caused. His wife and children, his friends and coworkers are all affected by the unmitigated drinking. He lost his license after multiple DUIs and can barely keep a job. After his wife left him, he decided to try and drink his life away. The pain he carried for years was too much to bear, and the shame of his addiction was coming to a head. Something had to change, or he was going to kill himself.

This is a picture of a wretch. It's a person who recognizes the mess he has gotten himself into. He sees the culmination of choices that were intended to numb the pain of his trauma and abuse. He knows he can't get out of this mess alone. He sees it's time to reach out for help. Some call it hitting rock bottom. Whatever it's called, it's a point of discovery, but wretch is not a place to stay. It's a place to leave behind. It's a place from which The Father in Heaven wants his beloved son to depart and come back home. It is a place from which he is delivered, hopefully, never to return.

One reason I no longer embrace the sentiment in this hymn is that I am influenced by my role as a father of two children, who are now adults moving out and about in the world with their own hopes and dreams. They both had to learn how to navigate their own disappointment and hurt during their childhood development. I did what I knew to do at the time, and I certainly regret some of my parenting decisions. But I also look back on the lessons I learned after they left me behind in the empty nest.

After my wife passed away, I took to cleaning out the entire house. I went through every room, every closet, every drawer, purging the amassing of a lifetime of accumulation. When I came to my office desk, I pulled out several files and looked to see what they held. In the stack, I found the papers from my son's diversion judgment after he had gotten in trouble with the law. I looked at the date and saw it occurred thirteen years ago. I reflected on that time in his life and did what I think every other dad would do with that memory.

I threw it in the trash.

I tossed that manila folder into the bin, along with other useless papers, and kept on cleaning. What I didn't do was keep those documents to later review with my son so I could remind him of what a difficult teenager he had been. I never want to remind him of his past. He is so far beyond that now. And I never want him to relate to me from that point on as a teenager. I never, never, ever want to hear my son say, "I'm just your wretched son, Dad." If he referred to himself that way, my heart would be crushed. Instead, my desire is for my son to put that all behind him and believe there is no reason ever to bring it up again. We might talk about it as a memory but not as an identity of shame. I want my son to feel his rightful place with me as father and son. I want him to delight in our relationship of moving from child to fully mature son. So for a person of faith to boldly and proudly proclaim their status as a wretch tells me they are still stuck in the past, the past from which they have been liberated.

I cherish my role as an earthly father. To view life through this experience gives me insight into the One Whose Image I Bear. If I know how to give good gifts to my children, how much more My Father in Heaven wants to bestow on me the riches of his Kingdom in glory? Therefore, I should always picture myself within this metaphor of Heavenly Father and son. What are the names he has chosen for me? What are the identities he has adopted for me? What are his plans and dreams for me? If I see myself any other way than how he sees me, I grieve his heart. I do not picture my Father calling me a wretch, so neither should I. He's not yelling, "Wretch, get in here right now!" The Good Father doesn't do that, so it is completely unnecessary for me to see myself as anything less than through his goodness.

My past isn't meant to be ignored but it can be left behind. I need not continue to give it power by living in constant regret and shameful memory. Calling myself a wretch does not lead to an intimate connection with my Heavenly Father, and a secure, intimate attachment is the very thing my soul longs for.

Prone to Wander

Another phrase of difficult language is from the iconic hymn, "Come Thou Fount of Every Blessing."[2] It was written around the same time as "Amazing Grace" by a pastor and English dissenter named Robert Robinson. I remember singing it even as a child attending our little country Baptist church. It is so revered that I approach this section with caution and care. My point is not to tear apart such a long-standing favorite. Rather, I attempt to point out the way metaphorical language can limit the faith on which I stand.

---

[2] Robinson, Robert. "Come Thou Fount of Every Blessing," published 1758.

The fourth stanza states:

> *Prone to wander, Lord, I feel it*
> *Prone to leave the God I love*

Why does this make me uncomfortable? At first glance, I have to ask, "Why am I prone to wander? From whence comes this propensity to leave The Lover of My Soul, The One who Holds my Everything?" I'm fully aware of the metaphor that supports this thought. I'm puzzled as to why it has become so well accepted. To describe the sentiment, let me use the word: Loser. This was a metaphor taught to me as a young man discovering faith. I was shown from the text that I was essentially a loser until My Creator found me and forgave me for all the rotten things I'd done.

At the risk of hyperbole, I'm not sure there is a more important category of faith for me than that of personal identity. Accurately understanding who I am is paramount for a thriving life of faith. It goes way beyond what I do for work and my career path. It's rooted in knowing who I am as a person, regardless of what I do or how I contribute. Who am I as a son? As a father? As a writer? This quest begins as a child and is ideally guided by parents or caregivers who are attuned to the strengths, personality, and impulses of the youngster. But without attunement, the child is forced to learn their identity all alone. The child will look for validation in all the places that make sense until they find something that seems to fit, even if it is unhealthy.

I admire the work of Mark Laita on his YouTube channel, *Soft White Underbelly*. His premise is simple: interview all kinds of people who appear to be down on their luck and let them tell their story in their own words. Many of them are heartbreaking and tragically sad. He finds prostitutes, gang members, gamblers, and fentanyl addicts. You name it, he finds them. He starts every interview with the same question, "Tell me about your childhood? How did you grow up?" And in nearly every story, the problems can be traced back to the pain of early childhood neglect. The young woman who had never known her father, assumed that her identity was unwanted, and sets out to prove that identity to be correct by seeking out relationships that reinforce her feeling of being unwanted. This leaves her friends and family confused because they don't understand why she acts the way she does. Even if an intervention takes place, some wish she would just snap out of it and come to her senses. But the intervention is moot without the understanding of the identity that is motivating the behavior.

Years ago, I was in a group of coworkers experiencing a lot of conflict at work. I called in a consultant to help us figure out why. She was trained in the use of a personality assessment tool called The Predictive Index (PI). Its inquiry is based on how you answer two simple questions. The first question: *"Which of these words describe who I think I am?"* The participant is to circle all the words on the list that correspond with how they see themselves. The second question: *"Which of these words describe who I think people want me to be?"* And from the same list of words, they are to circle their answers.

After everyone took the test, I met with the consultant, and her immediate assessment was eye-opening. She showed me two graphs with the results plotted side by side to show the difference. In most cases of conflict, she said, the lines on the graph are opposite. She explained how people see themselves is often very different from what others think they should be. When personal identity and perceived identity collide, one will eventually win out. She described that when a person knows who they are and it agrees with who they think others need them to be, this is a condition of congruence, and the graphs look alike. She said these are the healthiest and most productive employees because they experience less inner conflict over their identity. I found this incredibly helpful in this process of resolving conflict. A problem can't be solved unless it is properly understood, and it helped me get to the heart of why the conflict was over the same old issues. We had been trying to solve arguments without solving the question of why they kept happening.

If I proudly sing out, *"prone to wander,"* what identity am I reinforcing? It's certainly not what My Father in heaven thinks of me. I see nothing in The Holy Text that alludes to this attitude. If I adopt this, it puts me in an incongruent position. Why would I take pride in an identity that assumes I will grow cold in my faith? I don't understand this eagerness to disagree with heaven.

I can't imagine any young groom pulling his bride aside on the wedding day and saying, "Honey, you need to know that I am and will always be prone to wander from you, even though we are married. You need to know that I will still wander after other women. And I confess that this is how it will be because that's just who I am." What is the young bride supposed to think now that her groom believes he will fail her at any moment? How long is this marriage going to last under the assumption that their love isn't strong enough to prevent infidelity? I've never known any wedding vows to include the confession, "prone to wander." This is the language of defeat. It flows from a poor self-identity and is useless in establishing an intimate foundation.

Prone to wander is a terrible identity to adopt. It is the presumption of failure cloaked in the armor of self-protection. It's an immediate denial of the power and possibility of intimacy. The vows taken at marriage are useful to frame the act of the wedding day, but they don't change the heart of the couple. No amount of commitment to "till death do us part" can stop a divorce. A commitment to developing deeper intimacy is a better antidote.

Bound to Love

I'm not comfortable with the tendency to want to believe that the negative impulses in my life are the most powerful instincts about me. The word temptation is spoken with the assumption that I am one step away from becoming trapped by my desires and ending up in a life of addiction. The darkness gets all the attention this way, and I'm not sure it's a good vantage point.

The apostle Peter gives a strong warning in his second letter about destructive influences against people of faith. He refers to a time when false prophets and teachers, who intend to deceive, will lure unsuspecting followers away from The True One and into a life of exploitation and oppression. He uses a comparison in the second chapter, "They promise them freedom, while they themselves are slaves of depravity":

> *For people are slaves to whatever has mastered them.*
>
> II Peter 2:19

The assumption here is simple to understand but always applied to a negative example. Whatever gets the best of me is my master. If I am overpowered by alcohol, I must eventually come to a place of admission that I am a slave to alcohol. Fueled by the pain of my life, alcohol provided an adequate and immediate anesthetic to that pain. Over time, as I continue to foster this master/slave relationship, I discover that I have become trapped.

A simple definition of addiction is *the exchange of self-control for the promise of a reward*. Whatever the compulsion, there is a basic equation that supports it:

> *Pain + Promise = Relief*

The sum of these personal factors yields the resultant solution. The wounded and empty heart is in constant search of relief from its wounds and will seek ways to soothe the pain. Even though pain can't be avoided, all pain needs to be treated and must not be ignored. It can be difficult for a nonaddict to understand the destructive behavior of their loved one. Their struggle doesn't seem to make sense and seems like something they could get past easily if they just wanted to.

I don't believe people are as dumb as they are shortsighted. Pain relief becomes a greater priority the higher up the chart it goes. A hangnail might hurt, but it is not that big of a deal. On the other hand, the discomfort of the toe after having stubbed it on the bedpost in the middle of the night is going to require immediate attention. Nothing else matters until that throbbing stops. And when desperation sets in, any form of relief seems reasonable.

To see a community of addicts congregated together in little tent cities in a blighted urban area is an incredibly sad sight. Such scenes elicit two very extreme responses. One is to try to intervene and do whatever possible to help these folks. The other is to assume they have made their beds, so they get to lie in them, and leave them to their own devices. The former is often addressed by throwing money at the problem. The latter is conveyed by a lack of action or involvement. Both are informed by a lack of understanding.

Any compulsive behavior is rooted in a reward system. Even procrastination has its own prize, and that is the ability to put off having to do the thing I don't want to do. I heard a woman describe her addiction to methamphetamines. As soon as she takes a hit, she is filled with the reassurance that everything is going to be okay. The euphoric escape, however fleeting, becomes worth the cost she is required to pay. In turn, she gives up her self-control to find that feeling of relief one more time.

When Isaiah prophesied the Chosen One, he described his mission of bringing Good News.

> *The Spirit of the Sovereign Lord is on me*
> *because the Lord has anointed me*
> *to proclaim good news to the poor.*
>
> Isaiah 61:1

What is this Good News? If we take it as a metaphor, consider what you know to be good news. Good news isn't something that needs to be explained and deciphered. Good news should be self-evident. It should sound good. But that's not really what I was taught. I was always told that The Good News is that my way to heaven has been taken care of and that I need to confess I'm a sinner and receive the gift of eternal life to ensure I won't have a future in hell.

I would call this the "kinda good news."

If good news was proclaimed to the poor, what sounds good to a poor person? Is it to know they don't have to go to hell, or is it to have enough money to pay the rent next month so they aren't evicted? Continuing on, what sounds good to these people?

> *He has sent me to bind up the brokenhearted,*
> *to proclaim freedom for the captives*
> *and release from darkness for the prisoners*
>
> Isaiah 61:1

What sounds good to the brokenhearted? What sounds good for the one in captivity? What sounds good to someone who sits in the dark all day? If the answers aren't directly tied to meeting the needs of the poor, brokenhearted, captives, and prisoners, then it should be termed Just Okay News. And I don't want to live with that anymore.

I want to believe in the Good News that sounds too good to be true. I want the Good News to mean there is actual divine power available to transform lives and set people free. Free from poverty. Free from addiction. Free from depression. Free from the generational curses that have landed them back into literal imprisonment. I want to believe there is an Advocate capable of exchanging a person's sorrow for abundant joy. I want to believe that this Advocate can comfort a mourning heart. I want to believe this Good News is real and not just warm sentiment. I want to know the Good News that can change the heart of an addict—the one that everyone else has given up on.

I'm uncomfortable embracing the language of always being *prone to wander*. To proudly sing that I can expect nothing better for myself than always being *prone to wander* from the One Who Loves Me Most does not require that much faith. If I firmly believe I will never escape from a propensity to do the wrong thing, I am ignoring the Heart of The Father, who always welcomes his children home. And isn't this the point of the whole relationship? Ours is based on a love that blows our minds. Our continued understanding and fascination with this love should draw us closer and closer, not causing us to want to wander from it. *Prone to wander* isn't good news.

Bound to love has a better ring to it.

The apostle Peter said that people are slaves to whatever has mastered them. I agree wholeheartedly with this statement. I no longer believe that the only things that can master me are negative impulses and desires. Imagine a community of people, by faith, becoming mastered by love, kindness, generosity. You would have a powerful example of Good News because fear doesn't govern them. They have become so intoxicated with the Love That Knows No

End that they will be forever strapped to it. Who wanders from this kind of place? There would be nothing remotely worth wandering from.

On the wedding day, the vows taken by the couple do not create a good marriage. Vows are taken so they can serve as reminders of intent, but they do not change the human heart to be open to receive love. No number of rules, guidelines, or structure will make a good marriage. If I were to put my money on one effort for a couple to pursue, I would bet all day on this one word: Intimacy. It is the opposite of wandering away. It is moving toward a desired end, which is always toward deeper, more meaningful connection with our partner.

Vows are not the safeguard. Intimacy is.

Intimacy is defined as close familiarity between two people. We have this longing because we were created with it. Our hearts and souls have the Imago Dei imprinted on them. Therefore, I must always ask myself, "How does the pursuit of intimacy look like My Creator, the One who gave it to me?" What does it say about the nature of the One who encourages close familiarity?

If I believe I am *prone to wander*, I will become bound to and owned by that belief. And as Peter wrote, I am a slave of that which masters me. Being confined by such small language binds me to the belief those words reinforce. And how do I benefit from this line of thinking? *Prone to wander* is a restricting viewpoint. It represents a negative mindset and will surely become a self-fulfilling prophecy. If I tell myself that I am *prone to wander*, I won't be surprised when I do. In this way, I don't hope for much more. I can keep my distance from My Creator and not feel the way I cause hurt.

Prone to wander is not the language of intimacy. It's the words of a person who has lost their place within their relationship. If a partner is *prone to wander* from the other, it's a sign that all is not well between them. Wandering implies coldness and a lack of intimacy. It's an admission of failure before anything ever happens. Even if a person has a track record of infidelity, the heart will eventually reveal its propensity. What is it searching for? What does wandering away provide? What question does it answer? What problem does wandering want to solve?

Within the vocabulary of current psychotherapy, *prone to wander* reflects a sense of insecure attachment. This condition is manifested in adults who have become so wary of closeness that they try to avoid emotional connection with others. They'd rather not rely on others or have others rely on them. This description does not sound like a heart full of affection for its lover. Instead, the closer two lovers become connected to each other, the tenderness between them helps protect the relationship. The awareness of what matters deeply to each other acts as a buffer. Drawing closer and closer reveals the secret places that need to be cared for. Intimacy lets the two lovers see each other clearly and feel safe within the other's embrace.[3]

And so it is with The Lover of My Soul. I don't care to be insecurely attached to the One Who Flung the Stars into Space. I'm not interested in wandering from the One Who Holds Everything Together. As I understand it, this intimacy is the very thing My Maker seeks with me. How can I not reciprocate? How am I not in awe of this gift?

The chief enemy of intimacy is dismissal. It disregards the glory, worth, and value of the partner. Intimate relationships fail when the needs of the partner aren't honored. Untended pain, especially from the family of origin, can lead to unmitigated conflict that goes unresolved. Unresolved conflict creates distance, and distance is the antithesis of intimacy. The catalyst of intimacy is the opposite. It is to draw closer, to be more curious, to discover and see more clearly the glory, worth, and value of the partner. And this doesn't happen unless both lovers are fully engaged. Instead of *Prone to Wander*, I prefer the metaphor, *Bound to Love*. The latter is what I long for and what I want to become. I'd rather be so overcome by the magnificent beauty of the love of My Father that wandering is the last thing on my mind.

Faith
That seems
Choked
And restricted
May only be
Root bound

The wrong sized
Environment
Will certainly
Stunt the growth
Of a thriving faith

---

[3] *https://www.helpguide.org/articles/relationships-communication/attachment-and-adult-relationships.htm#:~:text=Adults%20with%20an%20avoidant%2Ddismissive,have%20others%20rely%20on%20them.*

Faith
Forced to grow
In a tiny pot
Will never thrive
Beyond its container

The gardener
Might need
To shatter
The vessel
In order
To replace it
With something
Better suited
For your potential

If I live

And breathe

From a place

Of security

Not constant war

Would I be

Less defensive?

CHAPTER 10

THE NEW LAW

When using metaphor as a teaching device, it's important to appreciate the perspective of the audience. The Holy Text is full of examples of metaphors which I don't have experiential knowledge of but can decipher intellectually and surmise their meaning. Having never grown up in a monarchy or in a culture ruled by royal sovereignty, I don't know firsthand what it means to serve under the governance of a king. And when The Son of Man is referred to as The King of Kings, I can assume some of what that means, but bits of the metaphor will be lost on me. The same holds true with the metaphor of sheep and a shepherd. I've never herded sheep and I don't know their nature and tendency. But people who have can weigh in on the nuances and predilections that sheep have as creatures who need a leader and caretaker. They can speak with authority on a subject I don't personally relate to and help me gain their insight.

But talk to me within the metaphor of father, and I will feel what you say more deeply than through the terms king or shepherd. I was fortunate to be raised by a good father. I knew he loved me because he told me so. I am not unfamiliar with hearing these four words, "I love you, son." But many aren't, making the image of father very difficult to relate to. As a father myself, I get to interact with the metaphor of my Heavenly Father as I relate to my children. Thus, I will be naturally biased toward this identity.

The book of Acts includes a powerful metaphor that I don't connect with on a cultural or emotional level. As a modern-day reader, I need background and context, but the metaphor would make perfect sense to Peter, the one to whom the vision was given.

Peter had been going about the mission Jesus had commissioned him before he ascended. He was bearing witness to all he had seen and was traveling the region telling of the man who sets people free. One day about noon, Peter went up on the roof of the home where he was staying. As he was praying and waiting for lunch to be served, he fell into a trance and received this metaphorical vision. The text describes it like this:

> He (Peter) saw heaven opened and something like a large sheet being let down to earth by its four corners. It contained all kinds of four-footed animals, as well as reptiles and birds.
>
> Then a voice told him, "Get up, Peter. Kill and eat."
>
> "Surely not, Lord!" Peter replied. "I have never eaten anything impure or unclean."
>
> The voice spoke to him a second time, "Do not call anything impure that God has made clean."
>
> This happened three times, and immediately the sheet was taken back to heaven.
>
> Acts 10:11–16

This would be a pretty weird dream for you and me to have during a nap in the middle of the day. Being given permission to kill any animal, bird, or reptile on sight and eat it requires us to contemplate its meaning. But for Peter, it would be a difficult metaphor, not because he doesn't understand it, but because he does get it, and it cuts against everything he has ever known and held dear within his lifelong religious practice. Peter was of Jewish heritage; thus, he understood the laws that governed his behavior. There were rules about what he could and could not eat and with whom he could eat. This restriction was ingrained and deeply rooted. He might have even had a sense of pride that he had never eaten anything considered unclean by his tradition. Peter felt like he was doing the right thing and now was given a vision that would challenge his previously held beliefs about right and wrong.

What was The Advocate doing by giving Peter this disruptive metaphor that would alter his entire life and ministry? He was facing a major paradigm shift which made him uncertain and uncomfortable. He was a Jew, who lived according to Jewish law and custom and now is being told to scrap all that.

How difficult was this demand of Peter? I've heard explanations, but I don't think they go far enough.

Culturally, Peter was a Jew. And just like in any cultural legacy, there are those who are accepted and those who are not. In my home state of Oklahoma, I didn't know an African American until I went to college. The deeper racism I observed was aimed at Native Americans. Intolerance was both insidious and blatant but deeply prejudiced, nonetheless. Politics is no different. A deep cultural divide is now evident in politics and in the vehement anger that each party shows for the other.

I try to picture the weight of Peter's vision on all that he had ever known. He was a good, law-abiding Jew being told to scrap all his history and tradition and do something brand new. This kind of wholesale change is near impossible for anyone, let alone a man deeply entrenched in his birthright. Peter was being invited to a completely different understanding of his cultural reference point of dutifully keeping the religious law he had been doing his whole life. The Advocate was about to disrupt everything—not just what he would eat, but how he would view those his law told him were unclean.

Breaking the Law

The only concept of The Almighty that Jesus' followers would have had was bound up in legal understanding. There was an entire religious legal system dedicated to enforcing the laws that God handed down to Moses. To obey God was to follow his laws. Keep the law and avoid the wrath. Break the law and risk banishment, or worse, sudden death. It's all they knew; therefore, their faith was defined within these limited boundaries. By faith, keep the law, and everything will be okay for you and your family.

Peter was given the vision of a sheet lowered from heaven three times. On this sheet were all kinds of animals, many of which were forbidden for him to eat because of the dietary restrictions outlined within his cultural laws. These animals were considered unclean. And his entire life, he had never eaten anything unclean. Imagine Peter's ambivalence when he was told that it's okay to eat anything on this sheet. This is more than the lifelong vegetarian being encouraged to eat a beefsteak. Most vegetarians in my culture limit their diet by choice, not legal restrictions. It's very difficult to convey with a metaphor just how conflicting this instruction would have been. It might be like being told that it's okay to eat a bald eagle along with that fried chicken. The eagle is a protected species. It's against US law to kill one, let alone eat it. Doing so could bring as much as a $100,000 fine and a year in prison. United States citizens have a common-sense understanding that bald eagles are off limits. If an avid bird hunter is suddenly told over lunch one day that bald eagles are now in season, this hunter is going to think twice about the source of this new information. The hunter is very familiar with the laws protecting this national symbol. Peter was being told to break the law. It's no wonder The Advocate gave the vision three times. The Advocate needed to reinforce the importance of the new permission. But it still took a while for it to sink in.

At the time of this vision, three men arrived at the house where Peter was staying and asked to see him. The men were sent by a centurion named Cornelius. He held a position of authority among a company of soldiers called the Italian Regiment. He was generous to those in need, a God-fearing man who prayed regularly. In response to his generosity and prayer, The Advocate sent an angel who instructed Cornelius to send for a man named Peter. The text doesn't indicate exactly what Cornelius was praying for but implies that Peter will deliver the answer.

What complicates the story is that Cornelius is a Gentile. This is a very significant detail to include in this story because Cornelius was not a Jew. It was against the law for Peter to associate with or enter the house of a non-Jewish person. He reminds Cornelius of this fact:

> He said to them: "You are well aware that it is against our law for a Jew to associate with or visit a Gentile. But God has shown me that I should not call anyone impure or unclean.
>
> Acts 10:28

This is an incredible narrative of what The Advocate does to engage his people in telling the Good News of the Son of Man in the most unlikely ways. It's possible to underestimate and miss the magnitude of the paradigm shift that Peter had to undergo in a matter of hours. Peter had to come to terms with being told it was permissible to break two major laws—two laws that were very basic to all Jews. Suddenly, everything unclean was no longer forbidden and every non-Jewish person was no longer to be avoided. It's easy for a modern-day reader to miss the profundity of this endorsement.

Was Peter really being told to break the law? Was this instruction temporary and just limited to this one incident? Or was he part of ushering in a revolutionary change from reliance on the law to relationship with The Advocate?

The New Law

Laws bring order. Laws are set in place to minimize chaos among social systems. They are very useful in creating an orderly community. But laws don't change citizens or convince them to do what the law says. Neither does punishment deter the behavior of a person bent on doing what they please. Laws cannot change the heart of an individual.

Keeping the religious law was ingrained into Peter's life. Through this law, he knew what was expected of him and he behaved consistently and faithfully. But a noonday apocalypse was unfolding, one that would require new faith to embrace and act upon. The Advocate was instructing Peter to forgo his past performance which was dictated by following a law and trusting a completely new era that was unfolding. From this day forward, following and embracing The Advocate would be Peter's primary concern.

This is monumental and a dangerous thought to entertain. Anytime we are asking for change, the hearers of the message will naturally assume what they have been doing is all wrong. This reticence is what makes it so difficult to convince people to change their ways. So back to our question: Was The Advocate actually telling Peter to break the law?

To this, I would say no. The instruction was not to override a couple of laws for the sake of a special appointment and then go back to business as usual. This kind of thinking is far too small for a life devoted to following The Advocate. The invitation to Peter went a step further. Life with The Advocate is always moving forward and never backward. Peter would never have to return to an old system. The law would no longer serve as the judge and jury of a life of faith. The Advocate would take up that role. The Advocate would convict a person of sin, not the law. The Advocate would point out where a person has it wrong. The once-revered law would step aside in order for The Advocate to take up a brand-new role. This new paradigm is intimately connected to the heart and soul of a person of faith. And Peter was the forerunner of this invitation. He was being invited to relinquish his insistence on the comfort and safety of keeping the law and learn to follow the voice and ways of The Advocate.

What are the repercussions of this invitation? Let me pose a thought.

As a law-abiding Jew, Peter would likely have prided himself in doing the right thing. Every social structure has norms and mores that point to the acceptable way of doing things. Remember high school? Remember what it was like to try and fit in? There were certain rules to follow. If you didn't, you wouldn't be invited to sit at the cool kids' table. While these rules were unwritten, there was an obvious sense of what to wear and how to talk. And if you made it to the cool kids' table, there were certain kids you should not associate with.

But some kids were different. They were the kids who didn't adhere to all this. They talked to whomever they wanted. They wore what they liked. They listened to their own music. They followed different compasses. They marched to the beat of a different drummer. They were not impressed by the petty status quo. They could and would relate to anyone.

This is how I envision The Advocate's invitation to Peter. He was inviting him away from the need to fit in through the law to become a person of faith who can transcend any custom, any lifestyle, and relate in kindness that goes way beyond the restriction of law.

I can picture the people within Peter's religious community that he was not supposed to associate with. But they weren't called nerds or goths. They were called Gentiles. And any non-Jew was considered off limits. You did not sit at their table. They were to be shunned and avoided. It's not hard to grasp how the racism ran deep. And this is one of many prejudices The Advocate was setting out to remove and making way for a new order of The Kingdom of Heaven.

As one would predict, word of Peter's unlawful encounter reached Jewish believers in Jerusalem. They were aghast that he would break protocol and enter the house of a Gentile and share a meal with these outsiders. But give the detractors the benefit of the doubt here. They were only operating on what they had been given. They were not aware of the new permission The Advocate had granted, so Peter recounted the whole story to them, step by step, explaining that the power of The Advocate was evident. It's as if he said, "What else am I supposed to do?" The text said this of their response:

> *When they heard this, they had no further objections and praised God, saying, "So then, even to Gentiles God has granted repentance that leads to life."*
>
> Acts 11:18

An unimaginable change was being initiated, and a cataclysmic movement was rumbling. The Advocate was now the new authority, and the old law would take a back seat. This would allow The Advocate to be free to rule the hearts of followers who had ears to hear. And Peter's encounter would start the avalanche that would disrupt an entire religious system. This wasn't a story of temporary suspension of the rules of the game, it was an entirely different game. Some would be hesitant to play. Surely, some were not so eager to believe Peter's vision that led him to break the law they had known their entire lives. Was it to be immediately rendered obsolete? What was to become of the Law?

As with all creation, it would be set free.

Law is restrictive by nature. It tells you what you can't do. It doesn't outline what is possible. In this manner, faith is not necessary. If law dictates behavior, then faith placed in the law requires keeping it precisely. Jesus came to set people free, not to give them a new restriction. The law limited what Peter could eat and whom he could associate with. The Advocate revealed that that era was over. The new starting point for Peter wasn't the law, it was the Voice of The Advocate.

Free to Be Free

Jesus' mission can't get much clearer than this:

> It is for freedom that Christ has set us free. Stand firm, then, and do not let yourselves be burdened again by a yoke of slavery.
>
> Galatians 5:1

Jesus came to set me free, which means he didn't take away the opportunity to return to the ways in which I wasn't free. I have a choice. His intention is that we become completely free. Freedom followed by a period, not by a *but...* To be free means just that: no limitations, no constraints, no restrictions. Freedom is the most critical condition for faith to thrive. If faith is to accomplish the impossible, it can't have a governor attached to its throttle. The law says, "NO!" Faith says, "Let's go!"

Freedom means I have permission to be foolish and permission to be great. My desire to accomplish the impossible by faith means I am also capable of ruining my life with bad decisions. I must have it both ways. If my faith is meant to thrive, it needs an environment that holds nothing back.

I must be free to make poor decisions if I am free to make good ones.

I must be free to waste my life if I am free to be exceptional.

I must be free to do nothing if I am free to be extraordinary.

This is why Jesus said it was better for him to go away so that The Advocate could come and encourage this freedom. The Advocate would be superior to the law and what it could not do. Authorization began abruptly with Peter and spread to those who understood how freedom works. When freedom is established, the real work of faith can begin. And under the wise guidance of The Advocate, all things are now possible.

Granted, the thought of this level of freedom can be troubling, but there is no need to fear the invitation of The Advocate, who will graciously guide us into all things great and wonderful. I can't imagine fear as an emotion that exists within The Kingdom of Heaven, therefore, it has no place for me on earth. I can't afford to entertain any thoughts that are not held for me there. The Advocate implies that there is no need to return to the solace and predictability of the law. The Advocate says, "I am here. I am leading you. I am comforting you. I am enough."

How can this be? How am I to live without the law? What will keep matters under control?

The Advocate.

But who will tell on those who are wrong?

The Advocate.

What will keep the people from constant sin?

The Advocate.

So what do I do with the Bible?

Read it. Revere it. Study it. Cherish it. Esteem it. Memorize it.

Just don't make a law out of it.

As soon as I turn the scripture into a law book, three things will appear: A lawmaker, a judge, and a punishment.

The lawmaker determines what the rules are.

The judge decides on the offense against the law.

The punishment is the price of breaking the law.

Whenever a law is created, a new generation of Gentiles is born. And this is a very dangerous scenario because laws separate people into two groups: the rule keepers and rule breakers. The rule keepers find superiority in the practice of keeping the rules.

Take these three statements, for example:

> *Therefore, I want the men everywhere to pray, lifting up holy hands without anger or disputing.*
>
> 1 Timothy 2:8

> *Women should remain silent in the churches. They are not allowed to speak, but must be in submission, as the law says.*
>
> 1 Corinthians 14:34

Make it your ambition to lead a quiet life: You should mind your own business and work with your hands, just as we told you.

1 Thessalonians 4:11

Who decides if these statements are correct? Are they rules? Guidelines? Laws? Are they all three equivalent in nature? Who gets to judge who is right on these three matters? And who metes out the punishment for breaking them? If they are laws, then who gets to decide the severity of the punishment?

Are the men everywhere supposed to literally lift up holy hands in prayer? What if they don't? What happens next? Who will enforce this law?

Is a woman supposed to literally be completely silent? Can they talk at all, or are they not supposed to utter even a word? Who will enforce this law?

What if someone isn't minding their own business and not working with their hands? Is working with hands meant to be literal or figurative? Who decides if a person is working with their hands or not? And what will the punishment be when a person isn't in compliance with this law?

Can I consider a different metaphor than law?

If I take these three instructions out from the confines of the law, what do they become? What if they were never intended to be a new set of laws? What if they are examples of the faith of the leadership on that day?

If I insist that the Holy Scriptures are a new set of laws, I end up incarcerating them. I lock them up and make the New Testament the New Leviticus. Jesus didn't just set our hearts free, he set the scriptures free. Combine a freed people with a freed scripture, led along by The Advocate of Freedom, and then faith can do what it was meant to do:

The impossible.

As long as I put a limitation on what The Advocate can and cannot do, I limit what faith can do. Faith of some measure might still exist, but that faith will never move a mountain. Forcing The Advocate to work within the realm of the law is to inhibit the purpose of fulfilling the law through the life and work of The Son of Man. To set free the beauty and majesty of the Ancient Written Word elevates the stories contained within it. It becomes more significant and more amazing because its nature becomes what it could never have been if it had remained a rulebook. Each morning, when I interact with the Free and Living Word, I get to approach it with an eye for possibility, not restriction. The language of the sixty-six books tells a new story of a thread of faith woven through the history of humanity by a Good Father who yearns for his children to come back home. He doesn't like the estrangement of his children, and he is setting everything in place to make sure we hear that invitation to be restored to him.

From Rulebook to Catalyst

Thanks to The Advocate, the book is finally liberated from its internment as law and set free to become a Catalyst for Faith.

There is a difficult concept used a lot within The Church as We Know It. It is the word "biblical." Folks use this term to indicate their respect for the Bible and a desire to study and determine what it says about a particular matter. They then commit to that position and call it "biblical." This is a valuable investigation if the goal is to seek out what will spur on faith as it produces love and good deeds. But if it is to determine how to be on the right side of the law, it falls short and is not rooted in faith. This is why I prefer using the word "faithful" or full of faith when searching the Holy Text for insight and wisdom. I might have a slightly different take than you on the matter of whether women can speak in church, but if The Advocate is leading us both, I don't have to worry about who's right and who's wrong. If our partnership with The Advocate leads us both to a response of lavish faith but with different conclusions, that sounds like a win/win to me. The apostle Paul pens it this way:

> *For in Christ Jesus neither circumcision nor uncircumcision has any value. The only thing that counts is faith expressing itself through love.*
> Galatians 5:6

Circumcision was a practice required by Jewish law. It was a symbol of being in right standing with the law. But the apostle downgrades this core tradition for the sake of something higher and more important. Faith is what matters now, not keeping an element of the old law. Faith that leads to more and more manifestations of love has taken over as preeminent to keeping the law.

Did the apostles believe they were writing a new set of laws for their followers and churches to obey? Did Paul write new laws for the Galatians? Did he craft a different set of laws for the Romans? Did Peter author yet another set of laws for the exiles scattered throughout the provinces of Pontus, Galatia, Cappadocia, Asia, and Bithynia? Were they writing the New Leviticus or were they, by faith, bringing order to the chaos of the young churches they were leading? Were all these laws compiled and eventually confirmed at the Council of Trent?

If the only thing that counts is faith expressing itself through love, I can see the scripture in a very different light. I don't have to study to determine the right way of behaving. I have permission to look at all the past ways The Ancient of Days has interacted with humanity throughout history and see what catalyzed faith into action.

What prompted the faith of Abel? Of Enoch? Of Noah? Of Abraham and Sarah? What about Isaac, Jacob, and Joseph? Or Moses, Rahab, Gideon, Barak, Samson, and Jephthah? How about David and Samuel and the prophets?

I want to know about the ones whose names we do not know. Tell me about the ones who through faith conquered kingdoms, administered justice, and gained what was promised. Remind me of the faith of the ones who shut the mouths of lions, quenched the fury of the flames, and escaped the edge of the sword. Don't forget those whose weakness was turned to strength and who became powerful in battle and routed foreign armies. And I am very curious about the women who received back their dead, raised to life again.

I am fascinated by the fact that others were tortured, refusing to be released so that they might gain an even better resurrection. I want to know about those who faced jeers and flogging, and even chains and imprisonment. Tell me about the kind of faith that caused some to be put to death by stoning and the others who were sawed in two and killed by the sword. Faith led some to go about in sheepskins and goatskins, destitute, persecuted, and mistreated, wandering in deserts and across mountains, living in caves and holes in the ground (Heb. 11:32–38).

Law-keeping didn't lead these followers to do what they did and to be remembered in Hebrews 11. I think this is why Paul wasn't that concerned with circumcision.

A catalyst is *a substance that changes the rate of a chemical reaction but is itself unchanged at the end of the process.* More simply, it is *a person or thing that precipitates an event or change (Oxford Dictionary).* I prefer regarding the Holy Text through this metaphor than through the classification of law. The Bible's intent is to produce change in my heart, while it (the Bible) remains unchanged. The catalyst of scripture changes me. I don't change it. A catalyst is disruptive. Its intent is to produce change. And if there is no chemical reaction when the catalyst is infused, it is considered inert, lifeless, and useless. If The Holy Text does not foment faith, something in me is defunct, which is what the law has already done.

If Peter were alive today, who are the modern-day Gentiles whom he wouldn't associate with under the law? Who would be considered unclean, uncircumcised, and unacceptable? Who would be ostracized and shunned because they don't fit the definition of what it means to be right and proper? And who would The Advocate say needs to be shown attention and care? Every social circle, every people group, every nationality has their form of Gentile, their very own personal Samaritan who does not attain. Wars are fought because of a nation's hatred toward the Gentile. Racism, segregation, and apartheid have been justified treatment of the Gentile. And dare I say, even The Church as We Know It struggles with its own Gentiles who don't abide by the law.

From Problem to Gift

Since the Gentiles will always be among us, it may be time for a different metaphor. Instead of viewing them as offensive, why not see them as a gift and not a problem? This was the invitation to Peter by The Advocate because Jesus saw Peter as a gift despite all his rash, impulsive behavior. Cornelius the Gentile was a gift to Peter, who was given a new name, The Rock, and the massive promise that the church of the future would be built on him and the foundation he laid. But it would require Peter to step away from his long-standing history, tradition, and security within the law. He was given the keys to unleash the Kingdom of Heaven on earth.

> *And I tell you that you are Peter, and on this rock, I will build my church, and the gates of Hades will not overcome it. I will give you the keys of the kingdom of heaven; whatever you bind on earth will be bound in heaven, and whatever you loose on earth will be loosed in heaven.*
>
> Matthew 16:18–19

Peter was convinced of who Jesus was. He knew Jesus was the Christ, the Son of the Living God. That wasn't his issue. His issue was with the law, and his biggest gift came via a noted Gentile named Cornelius, a man who didn't fit into Peter's law. The keys were the symbols of liberation from all the ways the law prevents Gentiles from being seen as worthy of the love of the Father. If it isn't locked up in heaven, it need not be locked up on the earth.

The only key
I don't have
On my key ring
Is the key
To death and hades
All the others
Unlock heaven

How would

This language

Shape my faith?

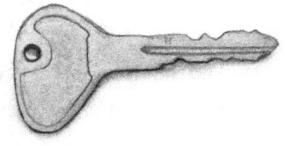

CHAPTER 11

SO WHAT AM I?

When I first began interacting with the Holy Text on my own, I was imme-diately confused. I tried to read it like a novel, and it didn't take long before I wandered out of the fascinating stories in Genesis and into the list of Old Testament laws and commandments. I was eager to learn about all I was discovering because it was all so new, but my eagerness quickly turned to discouragement when it stopped making sense. Committed as I was, I pressed on and kept going. I used the template of SPACE that I wrote about in Chapter 3, looking for all the things I was doing wrong in whatever shape or location I found them in the literature. I had no identity other than "sinner" because that's how I was taught to think about myself. All the passages about the wrath and fury of The Angriest One of All served to reinforce that I was to be watchful and fearful of that anger. In the beginning, I had no context for the two sections of the scripture. I just assumed that the Old Testament was part one and the New Testament was the sequel. In between was an intermission of about 400 years that I dubbed The Silent Years. In my mind, The Angry One must have calmed down, and people weren't doing anything to work up his wrath.

Feeling the brunt of anger was normal for me. I learned quickly how to tiptoe around angry people like my mother and late wife. I had a general fear of adults as a child because so many of them were angry, and I was the kind of kid who provoked anger through my humor and playfulness. Getting slapped, hit, or spanked was commonplace. And when I tell these stories to people who didn't grow up with this kind of treatment, the look of incredu-lity on their faces is telling. All of this produced in me a sense of fear and a need to become vigilant. I grew to always be on the alert for danger. I was in a constant posture of bracing for the next hit.

I was deeply ambivalent toward my new, angry savior. All I knew of authority was to keep my mouth shut and do what I was told. There were plenty of examples in the Holy Text to reinforce this status. But one story in particular rocked me for many years. It's a reference to Moses when he was being called to liberate the Israelites from their captivity as slaves in Egypt. I can still feel the anger of the preacher who delivered the sermon. He seemed to revel in the response toward Moses when he admitted he was reluctant to agree to the assignment. He camped on this verse:

> But Moses said, "Pardon your servant, Lord. Please send someone else."
> Then the Lord's anger burned against Moses . . . .
>
> Exodus 4:13–14

The preacher screamed, "The Lord's ANGER BURRRRRRNED against Moses!"

I can still recall how these words felt in my body. He said it with such vigor and delight, much like my math teacher looked when he yanked me by the arm out of my desk chair and pushed me out into the hallway, up against the lockers, and swatted my ass five times with his handcrafted tool of abuse.

What am I supposed to do with this? I'm a young man in my late teens, entering into a life of faith that is already very confusing. On the one hand, I am told that Our Father, who art in heaven, is loving and gracious, while on the other, he is full of rage and wrath against all the sin in the world. It would be another forty years until I got in touch with the abuse that was inflicted on me.

So, who am I?

I Am Always a Child

If faith is to be made available, it must be accessible to anyone, regardless of age, intelligence, race, level of education, or mental capacity. The Son of Man pointed this out when he referenced that his invitation was especially to little children:

> But Jesus called the children to him and said, "Let the little children come to me, and do not hinder them, for the kingdom of God belongs to such as these."
>
> Luke 18:16

At its most basic level, faith always starts as it would with a child. Children are innocent, vulnerable, and trusting. They need the love of a caregiver because they cannot provide safety and provisions for themselves on their own. Jesus acknowledges this in the use of the image of a child. He said children belong in his Kingdom because they possess all the essential qualities necessary to thrive within this domain. Even though I am an adult, I have confidence that I can always come to My Father with this childlike trust, knowing I will be accepted into his care.

In this way, I am, and always will be, a child.

This foundation of faith is critical for me to maintain because I will always find myself in circumstances where I do not understand what is going on and have no idea why there is so much suffering, chaos, and pain in and around me. In these times, a sense of childlike trust moves me toward Our Father in heaven, seeking consolation and reassurance. When I was a little boy, before I was able to read, I would sit in my dad's lap on Sunday evening and have him read the comic section to me. I had my favorites like *Blondie*, *Peanuts*, and *Beetle Bailey*. Dad would read aloud as I would decipher his words through the drawings. But there were a few comic strips he would skip over, like *Mary Worth* and *Prince Valiant*. These were not stand-alone comics but considered "soap opera" stories that followed a narrative that was built week after week. I remember asking Dad why he wouldn't read those to me, and he gave me the same response he gave to other difficult questions I might ask, like, "Dad, what's the Vietnam War?" or "What's Watergate?" I didn't understand it then, but I understand now why he always replied:

"It's hard to explain, son. You gotta pay attention."

I was five. I didn't get it then, but I get it now. How is he going to describe why our country was engaged in a war that cost the lives of thousands of young men and left many to return home injured and permanently traumatized? How is he going to describe the nature of a crime committed by our own sitting president? The best he could do was to reassure me that I need not concern myself with such matters and as I learn how to pay attention to current events, things will make more sense the older I get.

My Father in heaven holds the secrets of the universe, all the things too wonderful for me to know and too vast for me to comprehend. When it comes to these things, the best I can do is come to him as a trusting child and allow him to manage and take care of what only he can do. My part is to continue to grow with him in my understanding of what I can discern and enjoy. In this way, a child to a father is my most important metaphor. I can default to it at any time.

Jesus gave this word of thanks to Our Father in heaven regarding children:

> *I praise you, Father, Lord of heaven and earth, because you have hidden these things from the wise and learned and revealed them to little children.*
> Matthew 11:25

This word is my standing invitation to approach as a child. While all the wise and learned are deciding who is the antichrist and when the rapture will happen, The Advocate calls me in to learn as a child and receive the things revealed to me in this identity that would not be understood any other way. This does not dismiss the beauty of exploring heady theological matters. They are not to be overlooked or deemed unimportant. But they need not supersede the simple faith that a child displays in relation to The Good Father.

Consider the vulnerability of a child. When my first child was born, I remember the feeling of overwhelming responsibility washing over me. The nurse handed my son to me, wrapped up in his soft blanket, and we began to be introduced. This tiny little human being in my arms was now mine to take care of. I couldn't give it back. My life suddenly changed as I became a father. This baby needed my attention and the care of his mother. He couldn't do anything for himself except sleep and poop, and even these two functions required monitoring from time to time. But the boy grew quickly. It seemed like he was making daily discoveries that were fascinating to observe. He moved from being held to crawling, to walking, to running, to jumping from levels that startled my sensibilities. Eventually, he would learn to move himself with a vehicle. First the bike, then the skateboard and the snowboard, and ultimately the automobile. He was growing as he was created to do. It was my role as his father to be present in each step along the way to his maturity. He eventually hit some rough spots in his teen years, but he never stopped being my son. He needed a father more than ever, even though it was difficult for us to stay emotionally connected. He did not need my disapproval or need me to remind him of past behavior. He needed me, Dad, to welcome him into my arms.

The Good Father seeks a relationship with each of his children. He wants them to succeed. He wants them to develop their talents and minds. He wants them to grow in wisdom and understanding; but even if they don't, they will never cease to be his children. And this is why it is so important to believe the identity of a child is the baseline of my faith to which I can always return. The Good Father always wants his children to know they are welcome to come back home. They may be wayward or well-adjusted and highly responsible with the assignments he has given them. Either way, and regardless of age, his invitation is open.

The best way to ensure this is possible is to remove anger from the equation. Anger involves fear. Fear provokes shame. And shame destroys any sense of value and worth, the very opposite of how The Good Father feels about his children.

Unnecessary Anger

Another aspect of the metaphor of a child is the child's ability to perceive and absorb emotion. The love, attention, and support (or lack thereof) of its earliest caregivers will shape the emotional stability of the child's nervous system. If a child is raised in an environment of neglect, it will act out of that ill-treatment. If ignored, a child will act out in order to get attention, even if that attention is due to negative behavior. Being noticed is far better than being shunned.

Much of what we perceive about the world around us comes from our upbringing. If my parents were paranoid about the world being out to get them, it would be no surprise if I adopted that same paranoia. How I view my world is how my caregivers trained me to view it. This can be referred to as a generational curse. One generation passes on to the next what was handed to them. There is always the opportunity to change and go against the negative effects, but the strongest sway is toward what we learn from our caregivers.

Laws
By nature
Are limitations
Faith
By nature
Is infinite

Rules
Govern
Average behavior
Faith
Inspires
The impossible

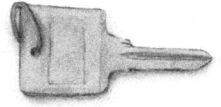

CHAPTER 12

WHAT'S A BETTER WORD THAN HARD?

Developing a Larger Language

Part of my motive for writing this book is to address the frustration with the language that was handed to me for expressing my faith. I learned how to speak about my faith, but I wasn't convinced it was sufficient to convey the depth and the magnitude of the kind of faith I hoped I could one day take hold of. The words, imagery, and ideas contained within my vocabulary have always felt a little small and lacking. It took a long time to convince myself, but I decided I should try to discover my own words and see if I could get closer to the beauty and majesty of the faith I find in the Holy Book.

I wrote a little poem that helped me in this pursuit. As with all my writing, I am my first audience. My reader is my secondary audience. It's like I'm taking notes from a conversation I am having with My Father in heaven first, and then I float the notes out for others to review. This metaphor helps me keep my focus in writing. If I make the audience my priority, what happens when you disagree with me, or worse, ignore or dismiss my words? I cannot hand off my reason for writing to a fickle source to mishandle.

This poem is titled *Use Fewer Words*, which became the title of my first book of poetry in 2021.

> *To be a better writer*
> *Be more honest*
> *Tomorrow*
> *Than you were today*
> *And use fewer words*

It seems counterintuitive, but in the process of writing to myself, I found I needed fewer words, not more, if I was to achieve a better language of faith. I set out to examine the words and language I relied on for so many years and am delighted in what I discovered.

Words matter. They are micro images acting as threads woven together to form a pattern of thought. This thought goes on to shape my belief about everything from what I think my world is like to the nature of my existence and what I think of myself. The thoughts become familiar and ingrained in my subconscious. Eventually, my persona and identity become so firmly developed in these thoughts that I no longer need to review them.

I have hesitated to use the word God in this project. I did this intentionally to force myself to communicate using different words. There are plenty of names to refer to The Almighty, so why not rely on the ones less familiar? How can I use fewer words to magnify The One I have come to know by faith? Can I go beyond the common and routine word God and reach a broader, richer sense of majestic glory that piques curiosity and spurs new faith?

> *The One*
> *Who holds*
> *The Universe*
> *In his hand*
> *Is the One*
> *Who longs*
> *To gather her chicks*
> *Under her wing*

My words can be restraining if I let them. So how else can I inch closer to describing the power and glory of The Almighty One without using superlatives? My language of faith should run the risk of sounding like hyperbole. My imagery needs to appear too good to be true—my vision of the better future, a fantasy.

> *Faith*
> *Loves to tell*
> *Stories*
> *That haven't happened*
> *Yet*

Words of Emphasis

The meanings of all words are assigned. This implied meaning is why I chose to limit the use of the word God in my descriptions and explanations. The word has a common familiarity, but I hope to move beyond the familiar toward new language that stimulates faith.

Take swearing, for example. The words we deem as cuss words have been culturally designated to convey a strong, harsh meaning. I remember as a boy saying the word *shit* out loud. I was confused by the appalled look on my parents' faces. I had no idea what I had said, but I was certain I would never say that word in front of them ever again. As a result, I learned not to use those words. And thus, I had a hard time with people who did. I gathered that swearing was wrong. I didn't understand it was not because the word was inherently evil but because of the meaning attached to it.

Wearisome Cross or Easy Yoke?

In my growing young faith, I was taught to emphasize certain words over others. Special emphasis was placed on negative language to describe the life of faith. One of the first Bible verses I was shown to memorize was Luke 9.23:

> *Then he said to them all: "Whoever wants to be my disciple must deny themselves and take up their cross daily and follow me. For whoever wants to save their life will lose it, but whoever loses their life for me will save it.*
> Luke 9:23–24

My leaders reinforced how difficult a life of faith can be. Following Jesus can be hard and costly. It can be compared to dragging a cross around every day. This cross represented death and dying and was a constant reminder of how hard it can be. But what if it wasn't hard? What if there was another way to define the act of losing my life that doesn't sound so miserable? What if I elevate my thoughts to a higher place so that when I face suffering or loss, I can see the reward in it?

But very little emphasis was placed on this idea, a proposition opposite of a heavy cross:

> *Come to me, all you who are weary and burdened, and I will give you rest. Take my yoke upon you and learn from me, for I am gentle and*

humble in heart, and you will find rest for your souls. For my yoke is easy and my burden is light.

Matthew 11:28–30

Which is it? Wearisome cross or light and easy yoke? Some would say it's both but that's where I disagree, especially as I search for larger vocabulary. If I emphasize the wearisome cross, I am fixed on a negative. I become enamored by what I am losing and what I am giving up, not by what I gain and become. There is truth to the cost of following Jesus. I must yield rights, demands, and preferences to walk with The Son of Man. But compared to all that he brings me, it's a measly comparison. If I am going to lean one direction, I lean toward the easy yoke.

Losing or Gaining

Joy was the prime motivator of Jesus' life and death on earth, as noted in Hebrews 12:

> *Fixing our eyes on Jesus, the pioneer and perfecter of faith. For the joy set before him he endured the cross, scorning its shame, and sat down at the right hand of the throne of God.*

Jesus was focused on joy, not the cross. From the very beginning, Jesus knew he was destined to die on the cross, and though it led through a most painful and difficult place, it brought him into a wide-open space of joy. To fix my eyes on the hardship of the cross will certainly weaken my thoughts. If I chose to put my focus on all I am giving up, I will certainly have an opportunity to hold on to those things I fear losing. But in doing so, I forgo the joyful rewards that await me.

Therefore, I am searching for a new language, one large enough to describe the joy set before us, so we don't get stuck in crisis mode and fretful, negative thinking. A quick search of news stories on the internet about the current condition of The Church as We Know It yields headlines and descriptions with a very negative focus. Here are three headlines:

> *Is the church too complacent in our time of crisis?*

> *Don't make the church leadership crisis worse.*

Who is to blame for people leaving the church?

Where is the focus of these headlines? What is the assumption? Whatever it is, it's all negative. Where is the joy set before us? These stories are stuck in the wearisome cross. We can do better.

Could it be that the Church as We Know It appears to be complacent because its eyes are fixed on the wrong metaphor? Could it be that church leadership needs to be in its current condition so that new leaders can see the opportunity to lead people of faith back to the joy set before them? Could it be that people are leaving the church because there isn't much inspiring them to stay? What if the next generation is saying through their leaving, "Can anyone lead me to the joy?"

Why does Jesus give us two seemingly opposing metaphors? My thought is this: some folks gravitate toward negative imagery. This angle makes more sense to them, and theirs is the Kingdom of Heaven, too. When we are outside of the law, The Advocate relates to his children as they are—just as I raised a son and a daughter. I raised them differently, with different instructions, guidance, and counsel. One needed a curfew. The other didn't. But they are both my beloved children, and I will do whatever I can to direct them with grace and wisdom.

Conclusion

Frustration was my initial compulsion to begin writing this book. I was frustrated by the inadequate vocabulary I had been taught about faith, but I didn't know if I could do anything about it. But frustration was not what I wanted to transmit. It's not what I wanted to highlight. I knew I needed a higher motive than discontent to keep me going. I knew there was more to be experienced and expressed than just adding another disgruntled voice to the existing cacophony of discontent with The Church as We Know It. It was upon a sense of abundance that I fixed my eyes. I didn't want to write a frustrated book. I wanted to craft a beautiful one. I wanted to see if I could find new language and metaphors large enough to contain the new wine waiting to be poured out and watch it resonate with a generation that still hopes in the creativity of The Author of Our Faith.

Frustration, like any negative emotion, can be a gift. It is the gift of invitation, bidding me to respond and do something about it. My response can remain negative and devolve into complaint and cynicism, or it can invite me to a higher place where I can contemplate a better response as I survey the landscape from an elevated vista.

Frustration is a form of anger, and I had to embrace my frustration with my faith as a sign of anger. Any kind of anger should never be ignored, or it will foment rage. And rage is never helpful. It is nothing but destructive.

My anger can lead me to abandon something altogether, or it can prompt a new inquiry. When I decided to ease away participating in The Church as We Know It in 2004, I did so in discontent. I tried to leave as quietly as possible and move toward a vision of a better future. I knew that if my faith were ever going to thrive again, I would have to give up something in order to receive something. I would need to make room for the abundance of faith I believed could exist. My faith was not going to thrive within a well-defined place. It would need a wide-open territory. It would need permission. It would need hope and love as guides.

David Whyte writes a beautiful word about the role of poetic language.

> *A poet's work is about creating a language big enough to represent both the world you inhabit and the next, larger world that awaits you.*[4]

I take inspiration from this quote, because I feel this commission clearly as a writer and a poet. I want to write about what I have seen and experienced during my short time here on earth. I want my work to be filled with hope and leave behind a sense of hopefulness that the best days are ahead, and that faith can prevail over fear and unbelief.

Even with this book, I must resign myself to the fact that I will never be able to adequately describe the vision of the better future that I have held for the last forty years. The language I speak and the words within it convey meaning, and oftentimes that language feels limited and inadequate to communicate with clarity. Four years ago, I discovered the language of poetry. This allowed me to retreat to a simpler language and use fewer words. It was a language that made sense to me. It met my frustrations as an outlet for expression and eased the angst in my soul fueled by a sense of inadequacy as a communicator.

What is my vision for the better future? What do I hope for that I will not likely see in my lifetime? What will be my contribution to the great cloud of witnesses long after I have taken my last breath?

I hope for a remnant of people who recognize that faith expressing itself through love is the most important work of all—faith that is not bound by a

---

[4] *Whyte, David. "A Larger Language for Business," by Lisa Burrell, Harvard Business Review, May 2007.*

previous rule or past law, faith that is free to dwell on making the impossible a reality.

I hope for a generation of faith that is above the law and not trapped by it.

I hope for a movement of faith that is kind, generous, and full of room for those who don't fit the parameters of a previous law.

I envision a quiet surge of faith that isn't easily identified because it is woven into the fabric of our cities, states, and nations. It can't be seen, interviewed, or photographed, but like the wind, its effects will be very obvious.

I imagine a collection of hearts becoming reacquainted with The Advocate and beginning to explore what is possible through The One who adores Jesus and was sent to teach and remind us of everything he said.

I can picture a revolution of peace, led by The One known as The Comforter, waves of peace washing over those who have been traumatized, abused, and broken by generations of unbelief.

I can visualize a new set of stories being told about how The Great Physician healed a generation of mental illness, disease, and other maladies once thought terminal and considered something to live with and tolerate with resignation.

All of this because of a cohort of faith liberated from the restrictions of law and set free to usher in the impossible for the sake of revealing the love of The Father.

I hope for a day when awakening is characterized by that word, as a generation awakens to brand new possibilities of faith because of an awareness of their deep personal identity as children of a Heavenly Father and not by their past failures to do the right thing.

I dream of a time when people of faith are consumed by the beauty and majesty of The Creator and not fixated on the worries of life's circumstances.

I believe someday in a Church of the Future that isn't plussed by what is happening in the world at large because it is too occupied with seeing thy will be done on earth as it is in heaven.

I know there will come a day when a person of faith will be so filled with the presence of glory and wisdom that people from all over the world will recognize it and want in on it.

All of this because the heart of seekers was so filled with faith that their longing for the impossible was more intense than worrying about getting it wrong.

In Benediction

May The Author of Our Faith
Join you
In writing a brand-new story
Never before told
On the diary
Of your heart

May The Advocate
Become your truest champion
Your greatest ally
And most palpable protector

May The Comforter
Fill you with easement
As you crawl under
The benevolent covering

May The Prince of Peace
Broaden the province
Of your soul
With ever-expanding
Freedom and abundance

May The Ancient of Days
Remind you

That all your days
Have been carefully planned
For you to discover
Transformation over improvement

May The Church of the Future
Show the clear evidence
Of the unmistakable fingerprints
Of your faith

Amen